RAISING THE RUNES

A Shamanic Journey through Avalon

Contact Jeremy to:

Book a Reading
Book an Appearance
Schedule an Event
Journeying Classes
Spiritual Counsel
Shamanic Teachings
Purchase Art

jeremy@jeremyrjwhite.com

For more information see:

www.JeremyRJWhite.com

Published by new72publishing
d/b/a new72media, LLC
19363 Willamette Drive #112
West Linn, OR 97068

info@new72publishing.com
www.new72publishing.com

Cover art, photos and internal art: property of Jeremy R J White.
Editor: Mary L. Holden
Cover design & layout: new72publishing

ISBN 978-1-946054-00-5 (p)
ISBN 978-1-946054-01-2 (e)

Second edition

Printed in the United States of America

RAISING THE RUNES

A Shamanic Journey through Avalon

JEREMY R J WHITE

PUBLISHING

For you mum.
I wish you could have seen this in print.

TABLE OF CONTENTS

ACKNOWLEDGEMENTS

There is appreciation embedded in this book for all readers of this wisdom that became mine to share. I am thanking spirit, the energy that makes all things possible, opens doors, and the eyes of everyone who opens to its power. This world we inhabit is full of magical glory!

I hail Odin. I give gratitude to the presence of Odin in my life and to let all know I am honoured to have this god walk every step of this beautiful journey with me.

To Tim Raven for his friendship and brotherhood.

The hours of support and friendship Kelli Lair has granted to me has been of great and everlasting value.

Thank you to my editor, Mary L. Holden, for upholding my voice as she practiced her craft with my stories.

FOREWORD

THE RUNES ARE A MOMENT of time, and also a thread.

The historical fact that this arrangement of sacred symbols and the body of knowledge associated with them survived over centuries is a miracle in many regards.

The characteristics of quantum physics, the toroidal magnetic field, and the multidimensional passwords to the divine source—all are encoded within these symbols. The runes involve both randomness and sequence in code and decoding.

The moment of rune energy is a representation of the momentum tunnel of life, on both the sacral and the sacred levels, within every dimension imaginable.

When cast, the runes provide insight, support, healing and growth for the individual and the collective that transcends linear time and reality as it is known. The runes are like a thread that has woven itself and stayed intact through generation after generation, linking us to our ancestors, to a distant past, predating what the church scribes have documented, and more importantly, woven us into a divine future that holds, for each individual and for the collective we call the human race, the embodiment of our highest potential as luminous, sacred and divine beings.

Some of the core components of this thread are the lineage of wisdom keepers, the mystical interaction and communion with the land we stand on, the sacred waters and multiple worlds that make up our universe. Those who have embraced the runic path have taken upon themselves the calling as land guardians, community leaders, healers and elders, and more importantly, as individuals, who quietly, humbly and privately incorporate these sacred symbols into their everyday lives. Through the simple act of pure intent, they have utilized the runes to enhance, enrich and empower themselves to fluidly and elegantly be woven into the fabric of our modern world.

As I write this, I am looking at three pictures that I feel embody these two main descriptors of the runes: time and thread.

The first picture, painted by Jeremy, is the same art that was the cover of this book's first edition. Selflessly given, as with so many other gifts Jeremy has presented us over the years, it is mounted on the wall that faces our family altar, with our ancestors' pictures facing the painting. It's in the very best place it could be. For me personally, and for my family, in our greatest moments of challenge, Jeremy has been there for us, and the runes have supported his loving acts of selfless intent, fulfilling his life's mission statement—to help those in need of healing and of knowledge.

The second picture is a photograph my wife Jennifer took of Jeremy and I as we walked through the redwoods in the mountains above our home. It was on this day that Jeremy walked into the middle of one of those sacred, ancient groves and touched the trees. He then turned to me and with tears in his eyes said, "Brother, this is your Stonehenge." The picture Jennifer took of us captured something very magical. In the photo, my 5-year-old son Brayan was behind us, looking at our feet as we walked. Jennifer later said that Brayan had spent the last five minutes imitating our gait and our posture as Jeremy and I were wrapped up in our conversation. Brayan was listening to and absorbing our words as he was embodying our gait, our postures, our rhythm as we walked.

The third picture, a photograph is from a day when Jeremy, Jake (my oldest son) and I hiked in the foothills overlooking the Pacific Ocean on the north coast of our town. Jake, at age 9, led our pilgrimage, chose the sacred oak grove, asked the land spirits for permission to enter and played his flute to honor the space. Jeremy and I just watched and held space.

Both of my boys sleep with a set of runes that "uncle" Jeremy made for them. Often at night, I will rattle or drum as the boys each journey on a specific rune as they drift off to the land of visions and dreams.

Moments of time, threads....

This book is really not about the runes. This book is a glimpse into a life, a collection of moments woven into the timeline of a man who has embodied the sacred teachings and wisdom of the runes.

My family has been healed, blessed, and supported by this man and by the wisdom the runes provided us, given with the purest of intent, with no expectation of reciprocity, the truest gift that can ever be shared.

We have witnessed the casting of the runes and the casting of those moments of time that we call a life, and by bearing witness to that trajectory, we have been blessed with the weaving of Jeremy's life into ours.

I recommend that you read these chapters from two perspectives. First, as a gathering of tales, to be told by the fireside, designed to take the listener on a sacred journey of healing and self -discovery. The second perspective should be one of anticipation and hope.

You may be tempted to step into the runic path, to start a quiet journey. Instead, leap. Remember, the runes are both a moment of time and a thread, and so are you!

We are the embodiment of timelessness, just like the runes, and we hold within us that sacred drop of the divine, placed there to help us manifest our greatest potential during our time here on this earth. Dance your sacred dance, cast your runes, become self -referencing and weave yourself into the timeless tapestry of our universe. We truly are the connectors of the past and of the future—just like the runes.

This book is an invitation from the runes and a man who leaped, who heeded the call and who is dancing his dance. It was said: "Come, take me into your hands, make your cast and dance your dance, weave your tapestry and rejoice in that part of the thread you were destined to be."

Did not Odin himself dip into that great well of timelessness, tethered by a thread?

It is just that simple, and it's been right before our eyes all this time.

As you embark on this runic journey through the sacred groves of your lives, remember the small child behind you, waiting, listening and watching with hope and innocence for those lessons that can only be caught–not taught.

With Love and Respect,
Bill Collins Francis
Santa Cruz, California
March 31, 2017

INTRODUCTION

*Cattle die, kinsmen die, no man is
immortal, but the things he does in his
life can live forever.*

~From the *Havamal,*
known as *The Book of Odin,*
or the ancient teachings of Odin

ODIN IS THE ANCIENT (ALL Father) god of the Germanic tribes of Europe and the runes are his language–the same words and sounds that echo within modern English. His stories–our tribal stories retold as modern fairy tales–their meaning is now completely lost. It is only when you look deeper and search for your ancestors do you find the real magic. J. R. R. Tolkien knew this and reawakened the sleeping ghosts of those who came before in his epic novels; it was the stories and characters of the Odinic sagas that inspired his mesmerizing tales.

My adventures with the runes started long ago, in a world that no longer exists, a world of lies, cheating, gambling and excesses of many kinds. It was in the darkness of these days that the runes called to me. They were a place for me to escape to, a place where I could see Odin and speak to him through the eyes and ears of the crows that watched over me from the trees. These mystical rendezvous I would keep secret from the rest of the world, for the characters of the pantomime I played in would never understand the spiritual forces that were calling me. It was when this house of cards collapsed around my feet and the very foundation of my existence was questioned, Odin and the runes came to guide me, to save me and show me a better way.

I asked myself a question: "Why am I writing this book?"

The answer is simple. Doorways were opened to me that have led to a whole new momentum in my life. A world of magic has been thrown before me and I had never seen a book that expressed this shamanic journey with the runes.

I could probably write a book about each individual rune. You can find a thousand different versions of their meanings by many different scholars. I am not a scholar, but I am *vitki* (a Norse medicine man). I live, walk and teach the word of Odin and these are what they mean to me.

Before going further, I want readers to know that I was asked to explain the meaning of each rune in this book. This request put me in a quandary. Many years ago, I taught the runes in a classroom setting. Although each student was amazed by the divination ability of the rune stones, they did not get to understand the true depth of each of the individual runes...they were studying them with their intellects, not with their own visions.

I did not want to write too much about the individual rune stones in this book, as I thought it might influence the way the reader experienced my book. As this is shamanic quest, I felt that others voyagers who are inspired by my tale would use their own vehicle of choice, but I know that I must say this: "Working with these symbols has been paramount in my shamanic development."

The example words for each rune I've written at the end of each chapter on a particular rune are at the simplistic level; 'tis my intent just to give you a taste of what each rune offers. You are not meant to understand the magical meanings—this is just a trigger to light your way.

I also include the way to pronounce each rune so you can chant it like a mantra as you use the words to unlock your vision. Note: On some of the runes an *az* has been added at the end. This is not the true pronunciation, but it's the best way to chant it in your own meditation.

Now, I teach the runes in a shamanic way, where the student gets to experience each rune in a guided vision before they know anything about the particular symbol I am teaching. This allows the rune to speak directly to the student and to provide a greater understanding of the stone's meaning. This way of teaching brings about a completely unique memory linked to each rune.

The runes are a language, an alphabet, a cosmic compass, a way of speaking directly to the gods and a set of keys that unlock the mysteries of the universe. Please treat them with the respect they deserve. Trust and let them guide you and do what the All Father directs you to do.

Here's what is important: Each rune has a mystical, mythical and magical connection and you cannot learn them all at once. Only very few initiates go on to understand the mysteries of the magical path.

The word *rune* itself means secret.

And some of what you experience on your path is for you alone.

> *Now, a warning: This book contains swear words and graphic descriptions. I apologize in advance if you take offense, but this book is an act of my personal expression and expertise. The Celtic people often use swear words as descriptive...and sometimes as insults. This language is familiar to me, and thus a part of who I am.*

This was meant to be a book about how to read the runes. But just as I finished it, I realized that this was wrong, so I consulted Odin in a vision. The wise one told me this book's intention is to spark your interest in the runes. Then you can embark on your own runic quest, your own adventure into the past and the origins of the tribes of northern Europe.

This short book will help reconnect that link to your ancient lineage. I would love it if it opened doorways and revealed mysteries to you, as working with the runes has done for me. Be bold, be brave, be especially open-minded and remember all the things you find upon the path of the 'blood twig,' an old kenning for the rune stones. Kenning means 'an understanding' and 'blood twig' was one of a variety of names given to the runes.

Every man or woman's runic path is completely different because it is an inward journey of self-discovery. The runes are keys that can unlock doorways to one's hidden depths and magical worlds. They see your secrets, recognize your fear and tap into your unknown potential.

ᛗᚨᛋ · ᛟᛞᛁᚼ · ᚷᚢᛁᛞᛗ · ᛃᛟᚢ

No man or woman's runic journey is right or wrong, better or worse than the next. It is just their story. So here is my story. Make of it what you will, but do not revere it as holy, or throw it away. You can use it as a tool to take the first steps on this wonderful path.

May Odin be with you.
Journey well, my friend.

STORY ONE:

GOLL ON THE TOR

W HERE DO I BEGIN THIS tale? I could ramble on about my life up to the time I discovered the runes, but that would be a distraction, like most of the things in my life before I connected to Spirit through working with the runes. I may mention the odd experience along the way, and of odd experiences I have had many, like the time....

After planning it for two years, in January 2010, my wife Tara and I moved across the continents to live in Glastonbury, England. We opened a little shop in the Gauntlet, bang smack in the heart of the old town, and called it The Crooked Woman. We were lucky to find a small but bright and airy attic flat just yards from the shop. It had fabulous views of the high street on one side and The Gauntlet pathway on the other. Having very cozy quarters, we kept our windows wide open as we slept and we were greeted every 4:00 a.m. by the seductive aroma of bread baking in the baker's shop across High Street.

It was at this time of day, as the bakers went about their business, that I would leave Tara fast asleep and head up to the Tor to feed the ravens.

Mornings are very special on the Tor. It is an ancient hill, which used to be an island surrounded by an inland lake, but the monks of the local abbey drained the waters centuries ago. This site has been a place of worship and pilgrimage for thousands of years and is regarded by some as the heart chakra of the world.

There is always magic in the air as dawn breaks over the Somerset levels. The ancient hill looms out of the mists—not just any mists—but the mists of Avalon. That is the long lost name of Glastonbury, the burial place of kings since time began, including King Arthur.

The same two crows—or ravens—always greeted me as I ascended the 600-foot elevation each day. These birds were sort of half way between the two species (you will find me calling them both names during this book). I fed them while I gave thanks to Odin and called in a blessing for the new day.

As the weeks went by, morning after morning, I could feel an energy growing. My connection to the land was waking something inside me, a long lost memory, an echo of the past.

One day, I was tending my business in our little shop and a burly, earthy woman came in through the door. She was wearing a cowboy hat decorated with feathers, a heavy poncho draped over her shoulders and she balanced her weight on an antler-tipped staff. We passed the normal courtesies then she asked me if I was the bloke who fed the ravens each morning on the Tor.

I told her I was.

"If possible, may I come with you tomorrow?" she asked.

I told her of course, as long as she was an early riser, and we arranged to meet at 6 a.m.

The next morning, we met at the corner of Well House Lane, where the path to the Tor begins. The fog was as thick as pea soup and we struggled to see each step that was ahead of us. It was going to be a long trek. There were hundreds of stairs, all at a very steep gradient. By the time we made the final turn on the approach to the summit, we were well above the mists and the whole of the town lay hidden beneath a mystical and vapory blanket, as if we were walking on the clouds.

Once we were at the top I called to the crows. By now I had given them names. Hugwynn was the bigger male and his bride was Munna. Out of the carpet of white fog the images of these birds appeared and landed near my feet. While I broke of pieces of bread for the birds and blessed the gods with each morsel offered, the woman spoke.

"I have not come here with you to feed the birds. I have come to show you something you need to see. To tell you something you need to know." With tears welling in her eyes she said "Can you see them, there in the mist?" she asked, and she pointed down over the edge.

Hovering and swirling in the fog were figures, ghosts if you like, hundreds of them. When I had seen a spirit in the past, only I had seen it. This was now to be changed—here in Avalon.

And, this was not what I had expected. I tried to focus on the horde that surrounded us. My friend found her voice again.

"You are descended of the Lords who lived here. Your ancestors killed all of these people and you are directly responsible for their deaths."

As I stared harder into the fog, one individual spirit came more into focus than the rest—a red haired woman. I had seen this ghost many times in my life, in dreams, in nightmares. She had haunted me since my childhood.

"Follow her. She will show you. Then you will understand and can start your true work here." My walking partner now beckoned me over the edge.

So I followed the apparition through the swirling mists and down the side of the Tor. Now to most sane people this must sound completely nuts, or as we say in England "a load of bollocks" but to those of you who have a touch of the shaman about you, it was just the average day.

The sides of the Tor are extremely steep and some of the way down I was sliding on my arse. Better to have soggy strides than a broken neck, so I cautiously slid my way through the stingers and thistles. Eventually the bank leveled out and the fog cleared. I could now see a well-beaten path laid out before me. The figure was maybe six yards ahead of me when I saw her come to an abrupt stop and stare out across the levels. I turned to face whatever she was distracted by and was struck by a draft of deathly cold.

The view I saw was from a long lost nightmare, from when I was a child, five or maybe six years of age. At the time, I woke screaming and repeatedly shouting "I can't move my legs!"

My mother rushed into my bedroom and asked, "What the bloody hell is wrong?"

I replied, "THEY," (although I had not a clue who THEY were) "have chopped my legs off!" It took several hours for me to be able to move my legs. The doctor, who was called, explained he could find nothing wrong and assured my parents that all would be well.

This horrific dream haunted me until I was about sixteen because it was always exactly the same. Here is how it always played out:

I was sitting mounted on a dark bay, wide-backed horse with other riders assembled. It was a damp cold morning and the smell rising up from my wet sheepskin saddle made me want to gag (that smell still sickens me to this day). As a group, we spurred our horses and charged down the side of the hill and into a nearby encampment. I was immediately knocked from my horse by a mighty blow that hit me bang in the center of my chest. Next thing I knew I was tied to a tree and watched with horror as two angry men, with utter hatred in their eyes, hacked at my legs with broad-bladed axes. Then as always, I woke screaming, sweating and struggling to feel anything below the knee....

Now, here I was in real life—on the misty Tor, standing with the red-headed ghost, and that dream of myself, from my childhood nightmares, again played right in front of me.

Then, the female spirit spoke not in words but communicated her message within my mind. Her soft but direct words filled my skull. "Remember this! You have lived here before. You were killed down there and your father and brothers massacred everybody in revenge for your death. You were your father's favorite son; no amount of bloodshed could quell the pain of his loss. So now you are to rebalance the crimes of your clan. Heal and help all you can to put things back in balance, to settle this debt."

She then turned around to face the path ahead.

The soft jingle of bells could be heard as a scruffy old man riding a caribou approached on that same path. He rode straight through her and onwards, passing by me. As I stepped aside, he turned his head to look directly at my face, smiled, then just continued on his way.

"He will be your teacher and his name is Goll." These were her final words. The ghost then turned and vanished back into the mists from whence she came.

This is how the knowledge of my ancestors now reveals itself to me. A spirit shaman named Goll comes to me in visions or dreams and shows me the ancient practice, the medicine of the runes, and how I must use it. I had used the runes for years but only in Glastonbury did they take on a greater, more divine importance. I am willing to share my experiences to guide you, but you must allow the runes to take you on your own spiritual adventure.

STORY TWO:

FEHU

THE ELDER FUTHARK (OLD FATHER) rune stones, the tools I use in my shamanic life, are the oldest form of this symbolic language. Opinions on their age vary amongst the academics, storytellers and sages. Some say they are a couple thousand years old and others say younger. I know in my bones they are much older, perhaps thousands of years older, and recent discoveries of runes carved into the entrance tunnels of the Bosnian Pyramids help to confirm my suspicions. Though many out there in the academic world think that this temple is a hoax, this book will not be an argument to change your mind. By your own free will you can come to your own conclusions. All I know is that this spiritual system is ancient.

The symbols, chants and talismans of the rune stones have traveled across the continents, having been scattered across Europe and North America. Runic inscriptions have been found on the steppes of Russia and several have been discovered across the heartland of America, including Minnesota and Oklahoma. The languages of Northern Europe have a runic origin. It is the intelligent language of our ancestors, who live now in our words, our stories, and our memories. It is woven deep into our culture. This language is a gift from those who came before us and it is our job to let the runic energies rise again in us.

Each of the stories I will share with you is given a name and takes its right place in the order of the runes, not in the order that each event happened. This gives you an easier trail to follow if you continue the quest after you have read this book.

I could wax lyrical about the academic meaning of each rune but that is not the purpose of this book. I will show you the magic I experienced through the doorway that each rune opened for me.

Fehu is the rune that begins these stories.

Fehu...and that red-headed woman. She is my female half in the other realm. For many years she scared the crap out of me, until Goll taught me to see it in a different way.

Once, in a vision, Goll came riding on his reindeer and sat down beside me at the council fire (this is the place of my teachings). We talked of the red-headed woman and my fear of her. He laughed and slapped me on the back. "You're afraid of part of yourself. Big strong guy terrified of a skinny girl."

This statement for me was strange because in my vision lessons I always feel like a small child.

"Many men have this problem, they think giving a woman power makes them weak, we are but two halves of the whole. Sometimes you need power and strength, sometimes cunning, patience, and magic."

(At this point, some readers may be questioning my vision. For those of you who don't believe in magic and sorcery, maybe the runes are not for you, for I assure you it does exist, and in many different forms.)

Goll beckoned his animal to come near the fire and told me to ride it to see what he meant. I climbed on board his reindeer. It was a very strange ride indeed. The creature had an extremely odd gait; it made me jig up and down like a pneumatic drill, until the beast had gained enough speed to leap into the air and fly.

Up and away from the Tor and the council fire, over the hills and valleys, back in time or to another dimension...I am not sure which. The caribou finally landed in a slush-ridden village; thick mud and snow were everywhere. The wary villagers were unwelcoming. They glared at me from the doorways of their rickety hovels.

I dismounted at a makeshift lean-to and tied his halter to a post. Dig! The sharp prod of a stick jolted my ribs and I suddenly turned to see another human.

"You a healer? Look like a healer. Chieftain wants you to take a look at his child."

I was back...back in time. The rancid furs that hung about this man seemed to indicate a time before written history. His language was coarse and guttural but I understood every word. As I replied, my mind thought in English but the words came out in his dialect. "I'll try to help if I can."

We both nodded and I followed the thick, shabby man up the slushy path. I could hear wailing from outside and smelled death hanging heavy in the air. We flung open the cowhide flap of the largest hut in the village. Most of the eyes turned to stare as I entered. Women were crying. A big man sat with his head in his hands.

"This is him," said my escort. "The healer."

"Leave us. Now!" The big man was up on his feet and had his hand around my shoulder in a flash. It felt like I was the answer to all his prayers. He shooed the crowd from his quarters and led me to the corpse on the bed. This child had been dead for some days...I could tell by the size of his swollen stomach. He had already started to decompose and the acrid odor ravaged my nasal cavities.

"I need you to heal my son. I have heard many good things of your work. If you help my boy, great riches will be yours and fame beyond belief."

"He is dead," I said. "I cannot help him. All I can do is make sure his soul makes it over the river, to the summer lands of the gods." I spoke confidently but fear was rising in the pit of my belly.

"You are a healer! Heal him or go with him to the land of the gods. The choice is yours." There was a certainty in the man's voice that made me shudder.

A rush of adrenaline flooded my body as courage left me. I tried to make a break for the exit but was grabbed by four big guards who hurled me back into the room of death.

"Best get about it, you have until dawn or your lack of knowledge will seal your doom, your reputation means nothing to me, shaman." The chieftain spit out these words then turned and left me alone with the boy's corpse, a fire, and a bubbling cauldron. The entrance swung open again and the redheaded woman was tossed through the door. The chieftain stood behind her.

He said, "If you need to make a sacrifice, take this girl as an offering to the gods. Her red hair is the colour of fire, and it will please them." The chieftain's face, although stern, had a glimmer of hope shining upon it. Did he think I could bring his son back? He left and slammed the door shut with great force.

For what seemed like an age, not a word was said between the girl and me. Then she spoke in a soft, yet direct way.

"So what do you plan to do? If you cannot raise the dead we're both goners."

I just shrugged my shoulders, hoped this vision would be over soon and I would be back in the modern world, watching an episode of "EastEnders."

"This will not end because you want it to. You must make a decision, one way or the other," she said. It was like she could read my mind. I was a novice from the future transported through the ages and into the body of a renowned medicine man. I didn't know what the fuck I was doing

Then she stood and took control of the situation, as it was obvious that I could not.

"Do what I do, exactly what I do, and be brave. You are not what you appear. Nothing is. Especially fear."

Standing in front of the boiling cauldron, she stripped naked and stepped into the bubbling liquid, beckoning me to follow.

She spoke as she gently lowered her body beneath the broth, no grimace, no sign of pain; nothing she did gave away her emotions.

"The cauldron is the womb of the Mother. We must be born again to be set free from this situation. You are a soul in the wrong body. If you wish to return to where you belong, follow me. There is no other option, for if you die in this vision...you're dead. Focus and understand. You are dead if you do not follow me! Come now."

I let go of the fear the strangled me, then I let go my fear of the girl and allowed myself to be guided, hoping that the cauldron would not hurt me. I placed my hand in the liquid and shrieked in pain as I pulled it out again. Flesh was dripping off my hand's bones. The pain was searing, a sense of horror washed over me.

"Do not be distracted by an illusion. Have nothing but total faith." She spoke clear and sharp, drawing my attention. Then I stared into her emerald green eyes above the boiling liquid and believed her completely.

I disrobed and stepped in, allowing the feeling to wash over me. The heat rose to my neck, clung to my face and engulfed my eyes. Finally I could bear no more. If this was an illusion, it was a fucking painful one. I let out a scream as the searing broth entered my mouth, throat and lungs.

FLASH...the next thing I knew, I was flung naked on the floor back beside Goll at the council fire. Born like a baby, shivering and wet.

"Did you understand that, boy?" Goll said as he sat cooking a sausage on a stick over the flames. I grabbed my clothes that lay at the shaman's feet, dressed and sat down beside him. It took a bit of time before I regained my senses as I replayed the events in my mind.

"I think I understand," I said to Goll. "Except I can't always be in charge of my own destiny, and there are some things that women know that we don't, pains that they can endure that we can't."

"There's a lot of things they know that we don't, and vice versa. Being scared of your female spirit can stop you from understanding many things. It will certainly stop your evolving into a medicine man. Embrace her knowledge. She is part of you. You have just been reborn from the womb of Cerridwen, and now you can really start learning. Oh, and where's my bloody reindeer?"

So there, that is how Fehu became the first rune story. Each of you will have a different beginning with the runes, some wonderful, some miserable. Both experiences have meaning if you open your eyes to the abundance to the lesson.

For me the first lesson was my connection to the female energy that dwells within me. I see this as a transportable wealth I can take with me wherever I go, something that I can tap into when my masculine mind becomes stuck or fixated.

Many years before this vision of Fehu, I was traveling in the United States and came across a Native American medicine woman. She took my hand and turned it over palm side up, she stared, looked up at my face and smiled. She told me that I would be a rune master because I had Freyja's rune (Fehu) in the lines of my hand. It was Odin who found the runes for his people but it was the goddess Freyja who taught him their magic.

FEHU (Fay-oo)
Mystical: Abundance/Cattle
Mythical: Goddess/Freyja
Magical: Dragon/Desire

STORY THREE:

UR

MY VISIONS, WHICH ARE SHARED in this book, are by no means the definitive expression of each symbol, just my psychic experiences brought on by the way my consciousness accepts the rune into my energy field. Wow! That sounds like a load of old codswallop, but bear with me. As this story unfolds so will the reason.

I was not going to write today, but whilst setting up my runes to help a client later, the Ur rune turned over. That is the rune that comes next after Fehu.

Ur is a difficult rune for me to explain in a vision. My experience with it calls up initiation and acceptance of my Celtic bloodline and finding my place on the medicine wheel of my ancestors.

Now is when I will introduce you to Tim Raven. He is like a brother to me. We both walk a serious spiritual path but love nothing better than taking the piss out of each other. It helps to keep us grounded and not disappear up our own backsides.

Our conversations are all about dragons, elves, demons, tree spirits and many otherworldly creatures. Most of the time, the passing Mug-bloods we come across, think we are both crazy. In my opinion, Tim Raven is one of the most gifted shamans I ever have come across and he walks a path of pure truth. He has a good name in Glastonbury—his guidance is of great value to those who live there.

This visions starts with Tim, Gary (another friend and gifted brother) and myself holding a drum circle at the base of what we called the "Hurn tree." This tree is one of the sacred trees of Avalon. It is a gateway, a portal to other realms. Note that the middle two letters of "Hurn" are "ur."

We began drumming, each of us playing a different beat.

I passed between the worlds almost instantly and found myself lost in a misty wood. I couldn't tell if it was dusk or dawn. In the distance I heard the bellowing of a bison. The call drew me closer and a white buffalo came in to view. I knew instinctively that this was a healing vision and wanted to lay my hands on its shoulders and place my forehead against his.

However, the healing energy flipped on me as the beast pounded the ground with his hoof and charged. I dove out the way, only for the beast to turn on his heels and start an episode of repeated attacks. Over and over again he charged, and each time I swerved to avoid contact.

A huge white stag appeared out of nowhere and joined in the assault. Together they took it in turns, rampaging towards me and chasing me, herding me like a sheep along a path. I ended up at a clearing where three young American Indian boys waited for me. They were no older than thirteen and dressed in white buckskins. Each youth held a different weapon, one a knife, one a tomahawk and one a spear.

They stood up and challenged me one at a time. Stepping forwards and encouraging me to fight, each youth came on. I defeated all of them easily, for they were just children and I was a full-grown man. When the last boy ran away crying, I heard laughter behind me.

The buffalo and the stag were now sitting around a council fire and beckoning me to sit with them. I felt like my ordeal was purely for their amusement, I felt ridiculed and angry as I took my place between them. Buffalo then passed me a large flat bowl and gestured for me to drink from it. In the reflection of the liquid, I saw a white bear staring back at me, and knew that this was me and I had found my role at the fireplace. I was white bear.

Looking up from the drink, I saw a white wolf sitting directly across from where I sat. I knew by intuition that neither the buffalo nor the stag could see this spirit. The she-wolf raised a finger to her lips and breathed a very soft "Shhhhhhh." Then she said to me, "Let this be our secret for now, for you need to find me and lead my way back to this place."

I woke from the vision totally exhausted, as if it had been a physical as well as a mental ordeal. My interpretation was that Tim was the white buffalo and Gary the stag and that my own source of healing power and strength was that of white bear, the shaman of the North. From that vision onwards, whenever I do any shamanic healing or am dealing with dark energies I take on the form of the polar bear.

The white wolf was interesting. I don't believe I have come across her yet. I am on a quest to find her, so the medicine wheel can be completed.

In conclusion to my vision on Ur, I was shown the source of my healing energy, a strength that I can call on to assist in my life and spiritual work. Whenever I go to visit with the Auroch, I touch on this healing energy. The Auroch were the ancient cattle of Europe. They were huge said to have been six feet at the shoulder. They represent the same healing energies as the buffalo to Native Americans. They are now extinct. In a vision, I go as white bear so Auroch will know me.

UR (ur)
Mystical: Strength/Energy
Mythical: Auroch/Ancient cattle
Magical: Primal Force

STORY FOUR:

THE RUNES AND THEIR PLACES

Now that I've introduced the first two runes, it is a good time to explain why there is a place that is significant to each particular rune. This is very important to me; it marked the realization that there were things I was to learn in Avalon that I could call on in the future, wherever I was in the world.

It was in June 2011 when I attained the knowledge of my runic map. I was doing some work with a group of American women, led by Signe Pike and Raven Keyes. As a culmination of what I had to offer, each woman was to receive a rune reading by me, performed at a sacred place within the Chalice Well Gardens. Except when I told this to Signe, she said that she wanted her to have her reading at the meadow below the Tor.

The two of us arrived at Signe's chosen venue in late afternoon and the reading went well. Then a figure appeared, coming across the field. By her red cloak flapping in the summer breeze I could tell it was Raven. She too wished to have her reading at this location. Signe thanked me and left to return to her lodgings at the Chalice Well Gardens.

I began Raven's reading. What came up and what was revealed in that reading can only be told by Raven herself.

Afterwards she sat pondering its implications as I cleared away my runic tools. I realized one stone was missing. We both searched for it but did not find it. Finally I told her it was my task to find it and allowed her to return to her lodging.

I had this set of runes for many years and was desperate to find the missing stone. After two hours of digging through the long summer grass, I still had not located it. I sat down in the last rays of sunlight and called on my spirits to ask for guidance.

Goll connected straight away, as if he had been watching and was sitting in the wings, waiting for me to call. "Empty the rest of your runes into your pocket, so they are loose and your fingers can easily stir them around. Take a vision walk to all the energy spots you have located here, places of vision, places of healing, places of darkness. At each site pull a rune from your pocket, look at it, and remember it and the location. Then cast it to the ground in a place where it will not be easily found. You must start from this spot and return to this spot when you are finished. I will be here awaiting your return."

I did as I was told and cast my remaining stones away. It was uncanny how, when picked at random, each one resonated with the site I left it. Finally finished, I returned to the meadow as the last light of day had faded. As I sat to reconnect with Goll, something hard was under my arse...a stone or ball of mud? No, it was the original rune I had lost. I was furious; it felt like a waste of time to have released the other runes!

Then I heard Goll speak. "Now it is complete. You have marked these lands with your runes, each one specific to a certain place. Wherever you go in the world, these runes will guide you directly back here to connect with whatever guidance you need. Now you must make another set, new ones, from the soil of these lands, to take away with you. That will be the final link in the chain."

He was gone as quick as he came. The vision made perfect sense and I did as he asked. My biggest worry was that I had several clients booked in for readings and had never used any other runes for my healing work, except the ones I'd just cast away.

The next day, I picked a set at random from my teaching runes. I always make my own runes, even for clients to use during workshops, and chant into them before they are fired. The day went well and each reading was as accurate as before. Although I did not connect with the energy of the new stones as much, their guidance was true. The previous set, now scattered across the lands, I had used in much of my own shamanic path and they had led me on many a sacred journey. Now they had been gifted to the spirits of Avalon.

The new set was to be made from local clay (mixed with soil from the Tor) and blessed by water from both red and white springs. This brings all the elements together:

- *Fire (the kiln)*
- *Air (the drying)*
- *Earth (the soil)*
- *Water (from the springs)*
- *Spirit (myself and the prayers said into each symbol)*

I anointed each rune with my own blood and made the sacred oath to Odin: "To say and do only what the runes show me."

This new set is the one that accompanied me to the United States. These are my traveling stones and I can connect with Glastonbury whenever I want.

So now we have the location thing sorted out, we can move onto Thuraz.

STORY FIVE:

THURAZ

T HE PLACE IN AVALON THAT is marked by my casting of the thorn rune Thuraz is a crooked old tree that has a loving, kind energy. When I sit beneath it, its sacred space is my sanctuary. Nothing can touch me there and I love that tree as if he were my brother. This tree I miss most—of all the holy places on the Tor.

There are not many times that I call on Thor in my vision medicine and when I do, they must be kept secret, but I will share a tale of a time I used it in the realm of men.

It was a fine Tuesday morning and I had just set up my market stall selling pendants and handcrafted items on the streets of Glastonbury. My stall that day was located opposite the Abbey car park. I loved those days being out in the street, mixing with the townsfolk, the tourists, chatting and giving advice.

This particular morning a strange, raggedy man appeared at my stall. He was tall, wiry, with a wild long and bushy beard. A haunting dark energy surrounded him, and my guard was up immediately. He wanted to sell some books to me, occult stuff, Aleister Crowley, and materials from The Hermetic Order of the Golden Dawn. These sorts of works were for those who deal in the dark arts, not me. The road I walked before spirit found me was about as dark as it can get, so these items were of no use to me; I had already been to Hell.

"Not my cup of tea, mate," I told him and then I explained that I was not interested in buying his books and suggested other locations he might try. I saw his focus shift to my top hat. He asked if he could try it on for size.

"No, this is my medicine hat; no one wears it but me."

This apparently was the wrong answer as he went off and started screaming. "I am Merlin, the true Merlin. I am the darkness that comes for you. I am the *spider* in the night to haunt your dreams." He ripped up his shirtsleeves to reveal bizarre alchemical tattoos.

"On your bike mate, I got nothing for you," I said. I was beginning to feel my old self rise up, the person who just wanted to punch this loony man's face. The skinny fucker spat on the floor, right by my feet, and stormed off at a wild and frantic pace.

About twenty minutes later, Tim turned up. "What's up brother? You looked a bit troubled, a bit pissed off?"

"Yeah, there is some fucking nut, walking around the town with bad, bad energy. Thinks he's the true Merlin."

Tim and I feel that we were and are spiritual guardians of Glastonbury, a bit like self-appointed psychic sheriffs.

"Alright, I'll go check him out and let you know what I think." Tim left in the direction of the high street.

He returned in about half an hour later. We caught sight of each other across the street and he was nodding his head in acknowledgement as he approached. "Yeah you are right, he is fucking mental. He has done way too much vision work and is trapped between the worlds. You see a lot of mad cunts like that round here."

"Guess what he called himself? Spider! Would you fucking believe it?"

"Then he must be test for you," said Tim.

Spiders always come in my dark visions because they scare the crap out of me. Lots of shamans believe them to be patient builders. Not me. When spiders turn up for me, the shit is about to hit the fan and it has never been wrong.

Over the next couple of days, I heard stories of several events involving this strange spider fellow. He had hassled young girls, caused problems in shops, smashed things and stuff and got away with all of it. In Britian it is called 'care in the community,' and it allows nuts to terrorize people and nobody says anything. It is a system where we should more compassionate to those who are mentally challenged. The idea is that we care for them in the local community and accept them as part of our society. Sometimes it works.... Anyway, it all came to a head in the assembly rooms at the monthly psychic fair.

Everyone in the town had been wary of him and the word was out to leave him alone; he was a bit touched, but harmless. Then, lo and behold, he walked into the fair. I was facing the other way but felt his energy immediately. I spun round and our eyes met. He changed his direction and headed straight for me. Beside me was a lovely lady named Julie and I told her to step away as I knew it was about to kick off.

Spider stood right in front of me and said, "I feel we have got off on the wrong footing. May I have your hand in peace?"

Trusting my intuition and not trusting this fucker as far as I could throw him, I offered my left hand (keeping the other fist ready to throw a short right-hander, if needed). I wear a very special ring on the index finger of my left hand that bears a fire agate stone, gifted to me by my wife. This stone repels evil.

The horrible scumbag spat on my ring and leapt backwards, as if he knew I was about to whack him. He started talking in tongues and cursing me. I felt Odin's power surge and take over my thoughts. I was speaking spells, cursing as well, chanting Galdr chants (ancient runic chanting) of destruction and protection.

People freaked out and backed away. Conjure up this image, like something straight out of *Harry Potter*, but it was happening. Must have been great entertainment for the tourists, but the people of spirit who witnessed this scene knew it was bad, bad shit.

Julie was really frightened. She called others to grab him and escort him from the building. As they dragged him from the room we were still at it. What I was saying probably translated in magical terms to "Fuck you and the camel you rode in on!" but to others we were both talking a complete mystical gibberish.

I knew spells had been cast because I felt one take hold of me during our altercation. He may have been mad but he knew his medicine. That night, his magic was to show its true dark intent.

I woke sweating at two a.m. to feel him, his energy, in my room. Then they came into focus and materialized before me: him and a horde of giant spiders. I could feel them on me, climbing on my bed, wrapping a cold sticky web over me. Fear engulfed my mind. Was I to die at the hands of a mad man's spell? Slowly I started to chant, to call in my magic, to awaken Odin within me.

The All Father came and gave me Mjollnir (Thor's Hammer) then spoke.

"Does this wizard truly mean you harm? If so, smash him to fucking pieces and have no regrets. For each man has the right to defend himself."

Energy soared through me. How dare he enter my home, my sanctuary? I ripped away the sickly webs, swung the mighty hammer scattering the spiders in all directions. The look on my attacker's face changed from pure evil to utter shock. He had no idea of the strength of my medicine or that Odin himself walked with me. His spirit image turned on his heels ready to flee. As he exited from the door the hammer hit him right between the shoulders sending his body tumbling down the stairs. I shouted out in a crazed voice. "Be gone from this town and don't fucking come back, you crazy bastard!"

It must have wakened the neighbors, but nobody said anything. Although I got on well with all of them, they were not quite sure of me.

Staying up, now pumped with adrenalin, I was fully awake. I cleansed my space with white sage and mugwort, purifying the whole area. Not a spider's leg remained, every nook every cranny was cleansed.

About four a.m., I lay down on my sofa and switched off my mind. I knew no rest would come while dwelling on the events. I slowly chanted the eighteen charms of Odin and drifted back off to sleep.

Some hours later I was wakened by a text from Tim: "Must meet for a brew." We met at Heaphy's, a teashop that was one of our local haunts for discussing all things magical. I ordered two cups of decaf tea, one with soymilk for Tim. (Soymilk. I can't stand that shit; it makes me want to vomit!)

Once we were settled at a corner table away from curious ears, Tim told me that at about three o'clock in the morning Spider was beaten up by some young gypsy lads, bundled into a van and driven down to Cornwall. He was then dumped on the side of the road.

I told Tim what had happened in the night to me. He had already heard about the dueling wizards in the assembly rooms, and thought it was fucking hilarious. (The Glastonbury gossip grapevine is sometimes quicker than Facebook). I explained that I had smashed the fucker with Thor's hammer and cast his energy out of the town. Tim thought that I should trust more in my own abilities and said that sometimes, "Some cunts just need a good bashing, and that cunt was sent for you to bash."

During these events I learned to understand the power of Thuraz and I never ever take its energy lightly.

THURAZ (thor-azzz)
Mystical: Boundaries/Defense
Mythical: god Thor/Attack
Magical: Dragon's claw

STORY SIX:

ANSUZ

When a stranger visits a hall of great men,
he sits quietly in the corner. He listens with
his ears and watches with his eyes so that
he may become wise too.

~from the *Havamal*
The word, the breath of ODIN.

MY LITTLE TALE ABOUT ANSUZ is once again set in the realm of men and was a lesson for me of another kind. It was to trust Odin–who wants to speak through me–for his words are sacred and not to be silenced.

I was holding a talk on the runes to help people connect and understand the origins of these sacred tools. The meeting place was in a room underneath the assembly rooms in Glastonbury (yes, the same place as the wizards' duel) but now we were downstairs and if any of you reading this book have ever been there you will understand. The basement of that place has, shall we say, a unique energy.

Well anyway, I was late and I am never late for anything so I rushed out of my flat and scurried across the busy high street. All of a sudden, a freak gust of wind blew up out of nowhere and flicked the contact lens out of my left eye. Crap! I could not find it without getting run over and after several cars had passed, that option was gone. I did not have another one to put in so I proceeded on my blurry path down into the classroom to present my workshop. I should point out that the vision in my left eye is not good with correction; without, it is about as much use as a teapot made of chocolate.

ᛗᚨᛋ · ᛟᛞᛁᚾ · ᚷᚢᛁᛞᛖ · ᛋᚨᚢ

As I entered the room, squinting in an odd manner, trying to focus on the attendees, I was taken aback to find the place fully packed. I would normally be at least twenty minutes early for any event, with time to set up and prepare myself properly to slowly acclimatize as the room filled up. This time I flung head first into the throng and was not able to focus properly. It set me on full tilt.

I stood in front of my audience, held my shaman's stick in the crook of my arm, and with my top hat perched on my head, I began to speak...but no words would come. It was like I was not there, not in control of my voice box. Nothing, I mean nothing came out except a muffled growl, like I was trying to clear my throat.

Through the fog of panic, a mist slowly appearing and swirled around the audience, a bit like the sad fog machines at the 1980s discos. The soupy mist came drifting up to the front of the room and engulfed my feet. "Oh NO!" I thought. "I can't have a bloody shamanic vision now!" No matter how hard I tried to ground myself, the scenario still played out.

Spirits of long dead Vikings were emerging through the walls, standing cross-armed, staring at me, waiting for me to talk. I was sort of stuck half way between absolute embarrassment about looking a total twat on one side and feeling an immense godlike presence in the room with me on the other.

I tried once more to push out some words, but produced only a wall of silence until a deep, guttural groan started in my belly and bellowed out of my mouth. This bizarre sound was not my voice at all. I now clutched for any lifeline that would give me something to earth my body back in Midgard, but none could be found anywhere. I felt totally detached from time and space. Then it came to me, the last resort, pass out and wake up in a hospital, to see a sexy nurse with a strong cup of tea for me saying "Never mind. Everything will be alright."

I could only imagine how uncomfortable this must have been for the crowd who watched, as I staggered, groaned and mumbled at the front of the room. They had paid good money to hear an educational talk. All they were learning here was what a fucking idiot I was.

Then one of the ladies in the front row spoke. She had silver blue hair and horn-rimmed glasses and wore an immaculate two-piece suit. In both her hands she clutched a shiny black handbag that was perched on her lap. "Go with it young man. I can see him, a huge spirit. Odin is trying to talk through you. Allow it to happen."

Another of the crowd chirped up. "Not just Odin, there are loads of warriors, I saw them coming through the walls."

"Me too," echoed a deep booming voice.

"It's fucking wicked!" a big biker at the back of the hall shouted out.

Now I understood. I could only see out of one eye. I had the vision of Odin and now he wanted to give me his voice, to use me to speak to the crowd. I had heard of this but I had never experienced it before, and this was defiantly not a good time for it to start. My whole life I had been a control freak and my challenge was to let go.

I sat back in the chair and completely ignored those who were gathered in front of me. I closed my eyes and shook the bells on my shaman stick as I went to meet with Goll in the vision world.

My shaman was laughing. "You look such a fool, like a chicken with no head, flapping your wings with nowhere to go."

"I know I do, well done. So what do I do about it?"

"Do you want to let Lord Odin speak through you?"

"No. Not here, not today. Maybe another time when I have prepared myself."

"Then tell him, talk with him," he said.

Then Goll was gone.

In my mind I called to Odin and said: "All Father, I am blessed to be chosen, but please return another time and I will gladly give over my voice to you."

As I imagined the words the process began. I felt his energy leave me, the control of my speech and my balance returned. The Viking spirits faded from the room back into the walls. They were gone with the evaporating mist and I returned from my vision, back to the classroom of mesmerized onlookers.

The first lady spoke again. "He has gone now; what a shame. It would have been wonderful to speak with him, to hear his wisdom. Did you send him on his way?"

Gaining my composure, I nodded to the woman and addressed my class.

"Yes I did. I have never experienced that before. It just threw me completely and I apologize to you all for my embarrassing behavior in this classroom. That was a 'Beam me up, Scotty' moment. Hopefully normal service will resume as soon as possible."

When embarrassed, always crack a joke. It's better to laugh with than to be laughed at.

The lady added, "He will come again. Not everyone can do what you just did—transmute. You were actually turning into him in front of our very eyes."

"Well to me, I feel I came across as an utter burk in front of a paying audience and can only apologize to you all."

For some reason unbeknownst to me the whole room gave me praise and felt what happened was totally authentic. That would only happen in Glastonbury anywhere else they would either call a doctor with a straightjacket or want their money back.

Back in charge of my faculties I resumed my talk and the rest of the session passed by uneventfully. Each and everyone present at that talk thanked me for an interesting experience.

Later on that evening I walked to my place of Ansuz. I sat and talked with Goll. He told me that I should have let Odin talk through me. There may have been an important message for one of those gathered and I had shut him out, shut out his wisdom and guidance. I felt somewhat ashamed of myself. I knew it was just a talk about runes, but what better place for Odin to speak?

I no longer plan to shut him out when he needs to speak. I (my conscious mind) will step aside and go somewhere else until he has finished.

Now here in America, I have met a gifted trance medium who channels the voice of spirit and it has given me the conviction to try again. She has shown me that whatever is said or happens has nothing to do with me. I would just be honoured that the All Father wished to use my humble voice as a tool, an instrument for him to play. If it happens, good. If not, it is not meant to be. I had a chance to really serve the greater good of spirit and I ran from it like a frightened child.

NEVER AGAIN.

There it is, Ansuz the voice of Odin, and I will always trust it and his messages and guidance for others.

ANSUZ (ansooz)

Mystical: Intuition/Speech

~~Mystical~~ *Mythical*: Voice of Odin

Magical: Dragon's breath

STORY SEVEN:

RADO

My visions on Rado have helped me understand deeper things about who I am and my purpose within this lifetime. Each of the many separate vision quests I have undertaken to venture on the mystery of this rune have always advanced me further on the spiritual road I now walk.

This vision I am about to share with you was only three years prior to the writing of this book. Like most of my visions, I cast the stones beforehand to see where Odin wishes me to go and what I would want to find out. On this occasion, my purpose was to release the emotional bonds that held me tied to Glastonbury so my journey to the United States could start.

Fortune had it that I drew Rado.

The place that is marked with the Rado rune is a gateway from where ninety percent of my visions take place (my place of journey). I sat beneath an apple tree and chanted the chant of the maidens, to protect my spirit whilst it travelled to the other realm. I called in the ravens on my shoulders, the wolves by my side and the badgers at my feet, each to watch over my body and call me back if need be.

I shook the bells of my shaman stick in time with my chanting. The sacred mists came and I slowly passed through them. I was at the council fire with Goll and other guides of mine. They welcomed me and asked me to talk on why I had visited them this day.

I explained that this moving on was for my wife, who longed to be home across the sea with her family. I said that I thought my own energies had prevented us leaving, because for the first time in my entire life, I felt like I actually belonged somewhere. I had finally found inner happiness.

"So what do you want from us?" said Tak Tara, my Native American guide.

"I need to know what to do to release the bonds that hold me to Avalon."

"What do you think you should do?" Goll asked while throwing a log on the fire and showering me in sparks and embers.

"I feel like I am happy to be stuck and I am scared of the future."

"The future comes whether you are scared or not. Just go with it, boy." Goll pointed at Tak Tara and the Native American nodded his head in acknowledgement, then he clapped his hands three times.

From out of nowhere came a black and white Pinto pony, with three big blue circles painted on its white rump.

"Take hold of the pony's tail and hang on for dear life or as long as you can."

I did as I was told by the old Native American and took hold of a good handful of its course hair. The Native American medicine man slapped the pony on the rump and the horse took off at a steady trot. This was a pleasant speed for a pony, a fast jog for me. Not knowing what was coming up beneath my feet added to my imbalance.

We rode through dark and shadowy woods, green, lush rolling valleys and over craggy rocks until it started to snow. As the snow settled, the ground became slippery beneath my feet. The path became steeper and steeper and I was losing my footing every other step. The horse finally stopped at the beginning of a glacier. I dropped to the ground exhausted, my sweat quickly turned cold and I shivered on the icy surface beneath me. My cramped fingers let go of the pony's tail, my arms hung limp beside me. This was when I observed an old battered wagon wheel, frozen in the blue glowing ice of the glacier. I knew instinctively that this, the wagon wheel, had to be freed to allow myself to move on...to set the wheel in motion, so to speak.

The wheel was frozen into the ice, solid. I tried to just use brute strength but it was going nowhere. I took my shaman stick from off my back, which was always with me, and began to chip away at the ice. Strangely, every time a large piece broke off, there was a flash of blue sparks and a groaning sound. Finally the wheel began to move—only inches, but it moved. I wiggled it back and forth, side to side and the ice fell away. With one final gut-wrenching heave, it was free and started rolling down and away from the glacier.

The wheel picked up momentum, getting faster and faster as it gathered speed. I ran behind but struggled to keep up with its pace. It splashed through streams, crashed through forests, jumped and hopped over rocks. It was now no longer in sight; all I could do was track in the wake of its path. We (me and the wagon wheel) travelled for miles and miles until the landscape became familiar and we neared the council fire.

Hollers and shouts preceded my return to the spirit guides. Those present were holding up the runaway wheel that had made a disaster of the council fire. I took my place at the disheveled camp. The guides who held the wheel placed it on the ground beside me.

Goll looked at me and said, "So you have set Rado free...to continue its journey. Strange! No matter how far you went in chasing it, it returned to the council fire. When you lost sight of your path it was us, your guides who held it steady until you could catch up."

The gathered spirits looked at me, and this time I nodded in acknowledgement that I understood the meaning of this vision.

Then the raven called, letting me know it was time to go.

I thanked the council for their wisdom and returned to the world of men, with a newfound sense that all would be well where ever I went.

Wherever my journey takes me, ultimately it will bring me back to the council fire. If I ever lose control or am unsure of my path, I know that my Guides are there. After all, that is why they are called guides—they steer my direction back to the right path. No matter how far from my true route I ventured in the past, events manifested to bring me back on track.

Each man or woman's path is the one they must walk. You cannot avoid it, no matter what.

So now I am in the United States because this is where I am meant to be right now. Even though I don't have a fucking clue what I am doing here, they do. My quest is to find out why.

Maybe it is to write this book or maybe to find the white wolf?

RADO (ray-doh)

Mystical: Travel

Mythical: Quest/Life's path

Magical: The Dragon's head

on a Viking ship

STORY EIGHT:

KENAZ

T HE SIXTH RUNE IS KENAZ. My site of Kenaz in Glastonbury is a place that takes me down into the underworld, Swartalfheim, to work with goblins and dwarves. Always on my path the answers lay in the dark places, hidden from view, and if I am scared to go there how can I find out the truth?

With this rune, as with many of the others, I will share a real life event. Or let's say I had one foot in each world at the time. This may sound a bit odd, but Glastonbury is where the veil is thinnest, which is why so many people glimpse spirit there.

The place I write about here has been sacred to me since I first set my feet in Avalon, or at least part of it, as there are two runes that connect me to the Dragon's Egg. Kenaz connects me to the lower part where I have to duck down and scramble in the dirt through the bushes.

One morning the ravens called me earlier than usual. I set off up the Tor, following my scared path. I fed the birds at the Dragon's Egg, said my prayers and made my offerings.

The Dragon's Egg is the High Seat of the Faerie King, Gwynn Ap Nudd, and you must find it on your own spiritual quest. You cannot ask someone where it is. Before you enter, you ask permission and you await a sign such as a bird's call, the bark of a dog, sighting of a rabbit or fox. You will know when it is right. If it is not right, then come back another time.

Anyway, I discovered this holy place and had made regular pilgrimages there to connect with Gwynn. I will speak more of Gwynn later in this book. So, back to the point, I had just finished feeding the ravens at the Egg, sat down and pushed my sacred knife into the ground. The fusing of the knife and the Earth creates the link to receive messages from the lower realms.

Gwynn's voice came into my head. "The dwarves are making a magical tool for you, a magnificent staff that will light the way on your spiritual quest. Dwarves are the master smiths. It is a great honour to be gifted something from them, for not all are blessed in this way."

I left this place and for some strange reason unbeknownst to me, diverted from my normal track and scrambled up the side of the Tor, to join the concrete steps, which is the path the pilgrims and tourists take.

As I made the final clamber over the long clumps of grass, I saw two Japanese or Chinese tourists coming down from the top. They were taking pictures. They stopped and we passed the usual common courtesies: "Morning!" "Nice day!" "Lovely weather we are having..." and so on.

Then the girl said, "Where is the most magical place on the Tor?"

Without thinking I opened my gob and blurted out, "You need to go to the Dragon's Egg." I was just about to point out the directions when a ball of dark brown energy came hurtling down the side of the Tor and knocked me off my feet and over the side. I tumbled head over heels, arse over bonce (a slang term for top of the head) down to the bottom of the mound.

Once the world had stopped spinning and things came back into focus, I heard a distant voice calling. "You OK?"

I raised my hand in embarrassment more than anything else.

"Yes OK. Thank you. Bye." I knew this was something to do with Gwynn and the thing that had bushwhacked me was goblin energy, so I hobbled back to the Egg, approaching it from the base. This was a time for me to be extremely humble.

Important note: Never approach the Egg from above...if you are so lucky as to find it. This is disrespectful and you will pay the price. Always come from below as a sign of respect for royalty.

From the base it is a bloody steep climb but I had to atone for my indiscretion. I sat beneath the bushes in the place of Kenaz and called on Gwynn and the spirits. They were not shy in coming forward.

"How dare you! Who do you think you are? This is a place of great learning, a power spot. Only those who are chosen can really connect with it. You choose to show just anyone." Gwynne's angry voice was booming in my mind.

Taking my reprimand like a naughty schoolboy, I sat in silence as the Faerie king bit my head off.

Close beside him were two goblins that giggled as I was chastised. The smaller of the two was definitely the one who had crashed into me from above. His aura was a muddy dark brown.

Afterwards, I understood that not all knowledge was for all people and it was not for me to decide who was worthy or not. Most of the world is not ready for the truth of things as I and other shamanic people see them.

Back in town I bumped into Tim. I relayed the morning's events to my Druidic brother.

"Fuck me, bro, that's heavy shit. Goblin energy is nasty stuff. They must fucking like ya, coz you only got ya arse slapped. It could have been much worse. I have had dealings with goblin magic and it ain't fucking good." Tim always spoke in plain English and got straight to the point.

I had much to learn about these lands, and these lands had decided to show me the truth. I must honour it and respect it. Now if I have clients who come with me for spiritual work, I will journey to Gwynn and ask for his guidance. Always give offerings and say prayers. Then, I always ask permission before I do any work there. And if is not right I don't do it. If he does not like the energy of a guest, I will take them somewhere else. In all my work in Glastonbury I have only ever taken four people to the Egg, all of which walk a path of truth.

Kenaz is the truth, the light, enlightenment. It is not for everyone. Some people can't handle it. Make sure they are ready for it before you ask for it to be revealed.

KENAZ (kennaz)
Mystical: Enlightenment
Mythical: The Torch/Truth
Magical: Riddles from the Dragon's jaws

STORY NINE:

GEBO

IN MY VISION WORK WITH this rune I have had many a profound journey—all of which I cannot share, as these were gifted to me alone from spirit. It is my contract with them to keep it secret. The significance of the rune can be realized in the 18th charm of Odin in the *Havamal* where it reads: "I know an Eighteenth which binds a spell and sets its purpose, which I will never tell to any man's wife or any young maid, except the woman I embrace, and perhaps my sister."

It is for each person who takes up a runic path to find their own words that bless a charm or prayer, as in the holiness of the word "Amen" to Christians. Your own sacred words will play a big part in your runic path.

I will share with you the relevance of my place of Gebo in just a short passage.

There is a site on the Tor where Druids and witches hold their ceremonies. It is a grove of Hawthorn trees, which is significant. There is a trilogy of trees in this place that are sacred to me, the first of which is the tree of Gebo. When I cast out the rune from my pocket to mark this spot, I looked up and the boughs of the tree were crossed in the sign of this rune. This for me was a confirmation that my path was true.

At that place I made my oath to accept the gifts given to me by spirit and to use them to help others. I gave thanks for the touch of the gods upon my shoulder and for guiding me in all I do. I cut my hand and allowed my blood to flow, to mark the tree, to seal the contract. There is no going back; a bargain was struck.

There are two things that can seal a deal: blood and spit. When I shed blood it is for a holy oath between me and the gods, an offering of myself. I have gypsy blood in my veins and when a handshake is made it is sealed with spit from the two parties. That is a contract, a solemn oath between men. "My word is my bond." So it is with Gebo, if you make a contract you must keep it, for what value has a man if his word means nothing?

If you've gotten to here in this book, you may think that some of my stories are utter bullshit. That is your prerogative, but what I wrote is how I experienced each event. Some of you may not understand how you can just open your third eye and dwell in two worlds at the same time. That is fine, but know this: I write with an oath made to spirit, to say what I saw in this world or the other and I come from a place of utter truth.

"My word is my bond to spirit and through the commitment of Gebo I connect with Odin and speak his words."

The statement above is extremely important to me, for before I found my spiritual path, I was a liar and a cheat of all kinds. Now Odin has found me and through him I see the truth–not any truth–but my truth. This is a gift the All Father has given me and I hold his word above all others.

GEBO (gee-boh)

Mystical: A gift

Mythical: An oath

Magical: Obligation

STORY TEN:

WUNJO

My WUNJO, OR WYNN, IS a rampant dragon on a red background and the vision I now share will explain how it began to heal me. Please bear with me in this chapter; by the end you will understand Wunjo and the nature of the importance of your flag. It is one of the key vision quests I take my clients on. It can be life changing when you accept its meaning.

Important note: Some of what happened within this vision I cannot divulge because it was a medicine just for me but what I have written has been approved.

I cast my runes for the direction my vision should take and Wynn came up. I already knew my own flag symbol, so I would visit and discuss with my guides about why it had appeared. I began to chant and shook my stick. I drifted between the worlds and into lands of magic.

The council fire came into focus and all of my guides were present, at least those who I had acquired so far on my journey. Spirit guides come and go at different times in your life. Some are to help and hold your hands through tricky situations. Others are archetypes for you to understand and help you evolve. This time I had 17 spirits gathered at the fire.

I sat opposite Goll as he unrolled a large deerskin in front of those gathered. Inside was my flag. He laid it out on the ground before me. I stared at it, not quite sure what I was supposed to see. I knew this image, however, because it was part of me. Then something caught my eye, and one by one, each of my spirit guides lifted up a cloak, a sleeve, a shirt, a trouser leg to reveal the same symbol tattooed somewhere on their body.

Goll cleared his throat and spoke. "All of us here have suffered a wound, for to be a healer you must have suffered a wound, of mind, body and soul. The sign of the dragon marks them of one of the brotherhood. Each of us, wear this flag upon our skin at the point where we carry our most severe wounds."

Gwyddion, a druid guide (a rough, tough woodsman type, I had picked up many years ago when I was drawn to another path), placed a heavy shaft of iron in the blazing council fire, sending out embers into the night sky. He looked at me with his strong kind face and winked. He said, "You are to be marked as one of us. Welcome brother."

All the spirits in turn repeated the same words: "Welcome brother."

My new brothers and sisters stood and gathered round me, congratulating me, patting me on the back. Instantly the energy changed. They took a firm grip of my arms and legs and laid me back upon the cold earth. Then the strength of their holds increased, which pinned me so I was helpless, to the ground. Goll leaned over and ripped open my shirt to uncover the huge scar I have across my stomach. This was the injury that nearly cost me my life, and led me to have direct contact with spirit for the first time.

Goll took the shaft from the fire, revealing it to be a branding iron, and a glowing red dragon shone through the darkness.

"Relax lad, you will thank me later," said Goll as he pressed the red-hot serpent onto my skin. A smell similar to that of a barbeque filled my nostrils before the searing pain kicked in, coursing like a tsunami through my body. "This is no quick fix boy. You must endure until he comes. Breathe deep and say your prayers, hold your focus."

I stared deep into my shaman's eyes and he stared back, fixing our glare. As the shaman held a steady pressure, he began to chant a haunting mantra, along with my gathered brethren. This chant you may one day hear but it is not for me to repeat in this book.

Somewhere between the pain, the smoke and the smell, a mighty dragon appeared and leaned over me. At this point, Goll released the brand, stood back and took his place with the others, giving the huge beast the appropriate space. Mesmerized by the dragon's gaze, I lay perfectly still as he breathed fire onto me, into me, engulfing me. Not a hot destructive fire but a cool, healing fire until the pain from my brand was gone. As the fizzing green light that shone around me faded, the dragon was gone too.

We all returned to sit at the counsel fire but now I really felt like I belonged among them. Nothing was said, just a feeling of acceptance. Slowly and quietly, out of the darkness, from all directions other characters joined us, figures from history, some of whom I was extremely shocked to see.

"You see boy, they are of the dragon, all of them. You too. Go now and honour the beast on your skin." Goll waved me away with a clap of his hands and I was back in Midgard, or the realm of man.

Totally invigorated, the dragon's breath had super-charged me. I ran home as if I was a teenager again. I vaulted gates, jumped logs and said a cheerful hello to everyone I passed. Back at the flat, Tara thought I was on some sort of drug or had taken a 'shroom or two with Tim.

I told her, "No, babe. I have to have a tattoo! Today, it must be today." Like a madman I frantically scanned images, all over the internet until the right one popped up, the image of my flag, my Wunjo.

This I am reluctant to share but I feel it is relevant to my story.

Wunjo was the image I had seen and accepted as my symbol so long ago. Now I knew that it was the sign of my brethren. The information I found said that this flag was the "Battle flag of Owain Glyndwr. He was the last Pendragon, the last in the blood line of Arthur."

I printed the image then added some runic symbols that had appeared to me whilst Goll was painfully marking the position for my tattoo.

The tattoo shop could not fit me in until later that evening, so all day I paced and recalled my vision, trying to remember every aspect of it. I wrote down and planned the holy chants that were to be said, as the tattoo would be marked on my skin. These runic chants would link me directly to spirit and the dragon.

"Isn't that really gonna hurt on that thick scar?" Tara asked. "Nerve endings can do strange things around scars."

"Babe, it has to hurt or there is no power in it."

I was positive that having this tattoo would be a religious and holy experience. I could not sit still, my whole body buzzed with excitement.

The time came at last and my lovely, supportive wife escorted me to the tattoo shop. I sat shirtless in the chair as the artist positioned the transfer of my sketch over my scar and began his sacred work.

FUCKING HELL!!!

I have had other tattoos but this one was complete agony, as if a pit bull was ripping my guts out. I struggled to remember my chants and when I did they came out as muffled, drool-drenched gibberish.

There are different types of pain and I have suffered. I have boxed, played rugby and been in more punch-ups than I care to or want to remember. The one thing that sticks out about all of these events is when someone hurts me I want to kill them and now I was looking at the tattoo bloke with venom in my eyes.

"Is he alright?" The tattoo artist said to Tara as though I was not there, or she was my mum.

Tara looked at me "You are OK, aren't you honey?"

"Just fucking do it!" I managed to stop myself from ending the sentence with "YOU DIRTY EVIL PIG! DOG!" Instead I just forced out and continued with my twisted runic chants.

One hour later it was done. As I stood jelly legged, the tattoo bloke gave me a lollypop. I looked at him like death and he said that it would help with my blood sugar. Supported by Tara, I left the shop. She seemed to manage to hold her laughter until we had left the premises and was out of earshot of the tattoo artist.

She giggled. "Oh well, if it doesn't hurt there is no power in it."

Her irony was lost on me. I needed chocolate, mead and "East-Enders." (For those of you who don't know, "EastEnders" is a British soap opera set in London that is religiously watched by most of the country. It is really good for numbing your brain.) Only then would the world be right.

I woke the next day and went to admire my brand in the bathroom mirror.

As I gazed into my reflexion, Goll appeared behind me. He smiled and whispered. "Welcome, brother." I knew now my path would take on greater significance from this point onwards.

There is immense power in knowing who you are: pride and a belonging. So discover your flag, wave it high so all can see and call those of your clan to you. For me this is the power of Wunjo. It is the greatest form of success to know exactly who you are and your role in this world. Well at least I knew who I was in the spirit world; my true path in this world was yet to be revealed.

WUNJO (woon-joh)
Mystical: Success/Joy
Mythical: Your Banner/Battle Flag
Magical: Fellowship

STORY ELEVEN:

HAGEL

MY EXPERIENCES WITH HAGEL ARE numerous and it would bore you sick if I were to recall them all. Instead I will cover the connection I had with the rune as I made my runic map, and one relevant event.

Each and every rune corresponds to an energy spot somewhere within Avalon. Each and every rune made perfect sense where it was placed...except Hagel.

I had just placed Ansuz in its sacred place and was walking away when I felt something bang on my boot. Another rune had fallen out of my pocket and landed near my feet. I had not planned to put a rune here but then it came to mind that the last three runes spelled the word HAG and as this was where I knew the local witches held their ceremonies, it felt appropriate. So I placed Hagel in this spot, where a thorn tree and a bramble bush made a low arch. I gave my blessing and sung the chant of Hagel to consecrate the ground. I then moved on. Only to find myself entangled in the thorns of the bramble.

As it was summer I was not wearing heavy clothes...just a bandana, a t-shirt and a cornucopia of necklaces and talismans, one of which had gotten snagged on the briars. At first, no matter what I did, it caused another thorn to attach to me and scratch at my skin. I cursed at the branches.

"Fucking 'ell, will you just let go of me!"

The bramble bush's grip weakened, as if it had heard my cursing and slowly but surely I untangled myself. As I made my way away from this place, ducking even lower under the arch, I asked the trees, "What the was all that about?"

A hush of a wind blew through the boughs of the thorn tree, "Ssshhhhhhhh," a sign to me to be quiet. As I rounded the next corner, a red kite came flying into view. Slowly I bent down and lay flat on the ground. I watched as the bird patiently stalked its prey. The red kite is a hawk and the hawk is the messenger of the ancestors. It brings us their knowledge direct from the spirit world. It is also the symbol of Freyja, goddess of runic knowledge. Hagel had delayed me so I could see this omen, to let me know. "There is always a reason for delay."

This is what brings me to me most recent event with Hagel and the reason I decided to write this book.

Coming to America was very painful for me. I cried like a baby when I left Glastonbury and again at the airport before I boarded the plane. My brother was with me, as he works for British Airways. He had come down to the terminal to wish me farewell. He witnessed my gibbering.

His exact remarks were, "What the fuck is up with you, crying like a girl? You don't want to go do you?"

I didn't reply to his question but he knew my answer.

We said our goodbyes and I boarded the plane. Then two hours later, got off again as the captain refused to fly it. The airplane had a possible fuel leak. So after another six-hour delay, I believe the land was struggling to let go of me (or vice versa). I finally took the great silver eagle across the pond.

Now living in the state of Washington with my wife, who was in sheer heaven to be home and around her daughters and grandson, I was in internal conflict.

My heart belongs to my wife but my spirit belongs to England, and Glastonbury. Here in the United States, I feel detached from my spiritual path. Back home I had been busy seeing clients, healing those who needed my help and they knew exactly where to find me. Here I was and am, like a leper, shunned by most. Even those I thought would welcome me with open arms went out of their way to close doors in my face.

My dilemma was how to survive financially, and more important, spiritually. I felt like I was dying inside. This situation could not continue. I had to do something about it.

So I visited my guides in a spirit journey.

Since being in this new land, it is not Goll who comes to me but Odin himself. Trying to keep a long story short (which I can assure you for me is near fucking impossible) I connected with the All Father.

I was back at my place of Wynn, standing by my flag that flew high above me in my Wunjo tree. I was briskly shaking the branches so that my spirits would notice me, when he, Odin, appeared. He was carrying a huge book, bound in rich red leather and embossed on the front cover was an image of the Tor picked out in gold leaf. The book was passed to me. For such a humungous journal, it was surprisingly light.

"What do you think it is?" The All Father asked.

"A book of magic. The book of Avalon, my Lord."

"Then open it and read it, for this is everything you have learned in this place."

I opened up the huge pages and was just about to read the sacred runic words when Odin pushed the book up towards my face. I was now holding it so close that it rested on the tip of my nose.

"What do you see?" He asked.

"Nothing."

"Why?"

"It is too close. I can't focus properly."

Odin then pulled the book back to my arms length.

He asked, "What happens now?"

"Things come into focus and become clear."

"So what is this lesson boy?"

Like a ray of light breaking through the clouds on a gray day, a beam of pure sunshine shone on me.

"I came to Glastonbury to attain this magic but I can't understand it until I am away from it. Only then does the medicine become clear."

Odin was gone and I was back from my vision.

I knew Hagel had risen up and grabbed hold of me. I am not seeing loads of clients because I am not welcome here. I am in Washington to get distance from my place of learning and to discover its implications in the real world. I have to digest that which I have been given and only then find my place here. I believe...wait, not believe...I *know* that writing this book is part of the process.

As my time in the United States has gone on, events have evolved to lead me into contact with two women, who I believe I will do holy work with in the future.

HAGEL (hagelaz)
Mystical: Delay/Storm
Mythical: The god Heimdall/
The Gatekeeper
Magical: Exhilarating crisis

STORY TWELVE:

NAUTHIZ

My EXPERIENCES OF NAUTHIZ, AT my place of Nauthiz are somewhat more unbelievable than my usual tales. I can assure that these events took place and happened in the day-to-day realm of man.

It was about ten-thirty on a Monday night and we had just spent the evening at the Rifleman's Arms pub listening to Tim play at a Celtic jam session. We were standing outside the pub. There was Tara, Tim, Silvia, her husband and of course me. Two figures approached from the town, heading in the direction of the Tor, on the opposite side of the road. Suddenly these characters made a beeline for us across the road, or should I say for my wife, Tara.

Both were Black guys dressed in North African robes and wearing sunglasses, even though it was pitch black out.

"You are a goddess from the stars," the bigger of the two men said. His companion stood silently off to the side.

Tim whispered in my ear. "I don't like these cunts, bro. Bad energy."

"It's alright, I'll deal with him. I think they are harmless enough or hope they are."

So I interacted with the travelers for a moment or two, taking their attention off my wife. We passed the normal spiritual chit-chat of Glastonbury and parted our ways. The two pilgrims went in search of enlightenment, to spend the night on the Tor and connect with its energy and we went home.

Earlier that same day I had had two runes tattooed in white on my forearms because of a vision I had, which I have written about later in this book. These two individual symbols are very important, for without them having been drawn, things would not have unfolded as they did. They have a great bearing on this story.

I woke as the sun dawned and could hear the crows cawing at my window. This always meant either one of two things: that I was about to have a spiritual experience or the crows were bloody hungry. Getting dressed, I grabbed a handful of food for me and some bread for their offerings, and made my way along the sacred walk towards the Tor.

There is a place in Glastonbury known as the Faerie Path and it leads to a field called the Jesus Field. As I walked along this Faerie Path, the morning sun cascaded through the leaves and illuminated the track with a breathtaking dappled light. Magic was certainly in the air.

Half way along the path there was a figure drawing something in the earth with a stubby stick. It was the taller of the two guys from last night but now he was decked out in some sort of witch doctor's regalia. This gentleman was adorned in beads and bangles. He was wearing a flamboyant colourful gown with African symbols and he wore a huge bell around his neck.

I recognized what he had drawn and I spoke. "Those are the two runes I have just had tattooed on my arms."

"I know sir. I have been waiting for you. Would you allow me the honour of blessings you?" The strange African man clasped his hands and bowed in front of me.

I trusted that this was no coincidence because of the runes he drew. I agreed to the blessing, as I believed it was a sign from Odin.

"My things are set up in the field along the way." He gestured in that direction with his hand.

I walked silently, trying to get some sort of hold on his energy. He mumbled a chant, in a strange unfamiliar tongue, as we went. In the field, he had set up a makeshift altar in the very center of the vast green pasture. A patterned blanket was laid on the ground with his magical items spread out around it. A strange assortment of bones, stones and bells, especially bells, fucking loads of them were scattered around the mat.

He asked me to sit in the middle of the blanket and focus on the stars beyond. As he swirled around me, he rang his bell and called to a celestial spirit of some kind. He asked me to spread my arms wide, look up to the heavens and open my mouth to let the energy of the Star Masters enter me.

I questioned the situation over and over in my mind because something felt very wrong. I saw him drawing runes—not just any runes, but the exact two I had seen in a divine vision—so this must be OK.

The bell rang louder and louder, I felt myself begin to drift into vision, when like a flash a bottle was waved before my eyes. BLACK SHEEP OIL is what it read on the label, as I got a fleeting glance of it. This brought me back from the brink of vision. It was like I had to be aware of what was happening.

I presumed this was the oil he used for anointing. Then with no warning, no permission asked, he poured a huge glug of it straight down my throat. Because of the position I was sat in, head raised up, mouth open and arms out wide, my first reaction as the oil hit my throat was to swallow and the liquid went down.

Instantly I coughed and screamed at him. "What the fuck was that? How dare you do that! You always ask consent before. You don't just pour some shit down someone's throat. You stupid bastard!"

"The Star Masters gave me permission, brother, and their word is final."

"Oh! Fuck the star masters and fuck you!" I was absolutely fuming and stormed off across the field, angry with him and myself for letting some fucking idiot ringing a bell poison me.

I kept thinking Black Sheep Oil, Black Sheep Oil. My mouth went numb, my stomach churned once, twice, three times and then I vomited into the ditch. Sweat was pouring down my forehead. I wasn't sure if it was from panic or from the evil medicine of an African witch doctor.

I struggled between wanting to run home and get Tara to the hospital or going to the Dragon's Egg. There I would call in my spirits to help me deal with whatever this was. After all if I have any real power in the magical realms, this was my place of power, my lands and my gods, so on I went, up the Tor.

By the time I reached the Egg I was shaking violently, cold and sweaty. There was no way I could climb the bank so I just laid in the grass at a small plateau at the base beneath. Flat on my back, I panted like a dog and called in my guides to help. I saw Goll and the goddess Brigit turn up and stare down at me before I blacked out and off into a bizarre vision, of which I cannot share.

I came round some time later, felt only very slightly better. Slowly and clumsily I struggled to my feet. As I did, a blue feather fell from my chest. This was to me a sign that what had gone on had been acknowledged by the spirits of these lands, where the land wights were watching over me. (The blue feather still sits in the brim of my medicine hat to this day.) I asked the spirits to keep me safe and help me make it through this ordeal. I trusted and had complete faith that they would aid me.

Slowly I wobbled, staggered and tottered my way down to the healing springs in Well House Lane. I drank copious amounts of water from both the Red and White springs, and then continued on home. I staggered into our flat, collapsed on the couch, gasping for air and moaning.

"Tara, Tara. Babe I've been poisoned by a witch doctor."

"What?" Tara was used to me coming in with bizarre stories but this one set her aback.

"Strong cup of tea babe, plenty of sugar." Tea is the elixir of life to any good Englishman. It is always the first thing we think of in any emergency. I played the dying man to perfection but was actually feeling a good deal better. Brigit's healing water was doing its stuff and flushing my system.

"Will you look up Black Sheep Oil? That's what the fucker done me with."

My wife frantically scoured the pages of the internet but to no avail.

"Someone must know what this shit is! This is the capital of witchcraft in the United Kingdom. There must be someone in this town who knows something about it."

After evacuating my bowels one more time, I set out on my quest to find the nature of my assailant's tool. This is one town that has an array of witches, herbalists, Druids and shamans, but none had ever heard of this oil.

I bumped into Tim and relayed the morning's events. "Fucking 'ell, bro, you've been tested. I knew that bloke meant you no good last night. What was the name of that stuff again?"

"Black Sheep Oil."

"No, never fucking heard of it. Why don't you try Star Child or Goddess and the Green Man?"

"Been to both bro, no joy. They have never heard of the shit either. I better go into work and tell them I probably won't be available for readings today."

"Let me know how it turns out, bro."

"Well if I'm not fucking dead, in the morning we'll go for a brew." Tim laughed and we parted.

I walked into Yinyang, which is where I held my readings in the town. Chris the owner, who was standing behind the counter said, "You look terrible."

I once again relayed the events that had unfolded that morning and said I was feeling a bit rough and only if someone were desperately in need of help would I go to work. He let me go.

Sitting back at home in anticipation of the end of the world, expecting any minute it to be my last dying breath, my phone rang. It was Lindsey, the co-owner of Yinyang.

"Could it have been black seed oil?"

"As I am dyslexic, it may well have been."

"Black seed oil is used by Buddhists to purify the body before ceremony, it will purge you."

"Thanks Lyndsy. Out of all the so-called specialists in this town you were the only one who could help. Bless you."

The rest of the day was spent between lying on the sofa and getting as much sympathy out of Tara as possible interrupted by bouts of lively bathroom action.

Two days later, I went to the White Spring to give a runic offering to the goddess. I heard the toll of a certain bell—something I will never forget as long as I live. There he was, bold as brass, ringing his bell and blessing the on looking, bewildered tourists. He was anointing them with the holy waters of the wells.

The rune I had taken with me was Nauthiz to mark that I understood my trial; that I had perfect faith in my own path and trusted them to protect me, letting go of all the doubt that would hold me back.

The African shaman looked up and saw me. His energy was totally different. The last time we had met, he had blessed me and I had called him all the names under the sun. Although I still absolutely believe that you do not pour something down someone's throat without asking first, I approached and handed the rune to him, blessed him for giving me a lesson but not for his previous blessing.

Tara had one more encounter with the African gentleman. She was inside the White Spring connecting to the goddess when she encountered him stark bollcock naked, cleansing himself in the sacred waters. This is an accepted ritual of many holy men and pilgrims who visit Glastonbury. They wash in the holy waters to purify themselves. She came back home and told me her story, which included the phrase "like an elephant," which I will not go into at this point. All I know is I my medicine is bigger than his.

These events led me to let go of my old self, to cut the ties that bound me, that held me back. In the Jesus Field I was born again and I could never turn back from my shamanic path. My old self was dead and gone.

"If it doesn't kill you it makes you stronger."

NAUTHIZ (now-theez)
Mystical: Letting go
Mythical: Essential/Fire
Magical: The Dragon's Fire

STORY THIRTEEN:

ISA

THIS STORY BEGINS WITH ME sitting in one of my sacred spaces long, long before I had designated a rune to each spot. I played my medicine drum, calling in Odin to guide me and show me that which I needed to know. I chanted the chant of the maidens and drifted off, beyond the threshold of the worlds.

There was no council fire, no gathering of brothers, just the Tor—bleak, dark and cold, engulfed in an icy blizzard. A shadowy figure approached me. It was Goll. He came so close that his forehead almost touched mine and I felt the warmth of his breath against my face.

"It is time for you to work within the powers of the white bear. Shift your shape, become him and wander. See what you discover. Go see what you can dig up. Use your nose to sniff things out." Goll faded back into the storm and was gone.

I looked down at my feet. They were not wearing the mountain boots I had put on this morning but huge white paws. Black claws were now where my fingers had been. I left the sanctuary of my body and walked away as the polar bear. Slowly plodding my path through the deep snow, I asked the ravens to remember my steps so that I could find my way back.

Cresting the backbone of the Tor, I saw three young men dressed in black and carrying torches that flickered in the stormy blizzard. Instinctively whatever they were doing felt wrong, so I stalked them through the snow, keeping watch on their activities.

On the north face they entered a doorway down into the ground, and as I followed in behind them, the door slammed shut. There inside, I was facing these three strangers; they were just young men. I was a huge ice bear. I stood tall on my hind feet and roared at them. They were not afraid, and in turn, lowered their heads, growing shiny jet horns, morphing into black bulls with piercing red eyes.

The first one charged me. One swipe of my paw sent him smashing into the rocky wall of the cave. Then the second and the third came at me. Each time I defended myself but I pretty quickly realized that eventually they would get the better of me. My eyes scoured the cavern for an escape route.

There!

There in the corner of the room was a rabbit hole. My mind was clear, if I could be a bear, then I could be ferret. As soon as the thought entered my mind I was small, sleek, swift and darting into the tunnel, away from my enemies. I heard scampering behind me. But not more ferrets.

Spiders. Big ones.

Now outside in the snow, panic struck me like an axe in my forehead. Anything but spiders! Taking huge leaps and then sinking in the snow, I knew they would soon catch me. Why could I not steady my mind and change back to the bear?

Then I knew why—fear had frozen me like ice.

The spiders seemed to be growing. They easily outran me. The first flipped me up in the air, and then all of them spewed their sticky web material over me, cocooning my body, perhaps for a later feast. Fixed fast within this tomb, I longed to be back in the world of men, down the pub with a pint in my hand, watching football on the telly. That world seemed a million miles away. Was I to be devoured in this shamanic trance? To lie here awaiting the spiders fangs to enter my body? Letting them inject their toxic venom and suck out my soul?

The world as I knew it was gone and the world of magic was dimming fast.

Crunch, crunch, crunch.... Smash! My sticky coffin was broken open and before me were two badgers. They were eating the spiders—snapping off their legs and chewing on them like a tasty treat.

I was free. Was I changed? The goddess Cerridwen appeared before me. She is the Hag, the Crooked Woman. She is Gullveig in the Norse traditions, but I was in the Celtic lands and she is the Earth mother of that place.

Cerridwyn said, "Everything fears something, boy. If we did not have fear then we would not last long. You fear the spiders. The spiders fear the badgers. Badgers fear man and his dogs. They are my gift to you; they are your brothers from now on. Take them with you on your visions. Know that they are always there when you need them. The crows will be on your shoulders; wolves by your side and now the badgers will be at your feet. One day the badgers may call on you to return the favour."

The goddess disappeared, the badgers finished chomping their meal of spiders and I returned to the world of men. Utterly drained and exhausted, I took it easy for the rest of the day.

That evening my daughter, Flissy, came to visit with her boyfriend Jim. They are both mad musicians. As it was the first Monday of the month, I took them to the Celtic jam at the Rifleman's Pub. Tim was there as usual and we talked of bad energy in the town, bulls, spiders and so on. My daughter had to explain to Jim that her dad wasn't really mad—these sorts of conversations were perfectly normal here. Jim was fascinated by it all.

We left earlier than expected as the events of the day had taken their toll on me and I was, to put it bluntly, fucking knackered.

As we meandered our way past the ancient twisting and bulging abbey walls, Flissy saw something big and fat in the middle of the road. This was a moonlit night and the silvery beams glistened off of the creature's black and white back. Jim was replaying on his iPhone the Celtic music he had recorded in the pub. The badger raised his long head and pricked his ears forwards to listen. His beady, jet black eyes were gazing upon us as we approached and he sniffed at the night air. The animal was unafraid; he just slowly got to his feet and wandered off, taking one last long look back over his shoulder. In that moment, I knew he was now part of me and I was part of him.

For me Isa is a wonderful rune. It teaches me to be still to sit and watch the world and to know that which I truly need will manifest. If the heart is true, the universe will provide. It is only when things seem the grimmest that faith is tested. When Isa appears there is to be a testing time for someone.

My place of Isa on my sacred walk is at a site of three trees, of three ages of man, youth, adulthood and old age, the three aspects of life that represent Cerridwen/Gullveig, the Maid, the Mother and the Crone.

ISA (ee-sar)
Mystical: Ice/Danger
Mythical: Stillness/Shaman
Magical: The Dragon's Gaze/The Void

STORY FOURTEEN:

JARA

T HE VISION THAT I WAS going to share with you was one in which Jara represented my return to Avalon. I had worked hard and was now to receive the rewards and joy of my homecoming. I had imagined making offerings at my place of Jara and giving thanks to the gods for guiding me safely home. Once again I was to feel the soil of Avalon between my fingers, and walk in the fields of my ancestors. Not so much as to be there forever, but to know where I belonged and to go there to recharge. I needed to receive a confirmation of my path and feel my connection to the gods.

For some reason as I started to write this, the spacing and fonts on my computer started playing up. It was all coming out in chaos and no matter what I did it would not correct itself. So I stopped my composition, sat back in the chair, asked Odin what was wrong with this vision I wished to share. His voice told me to journey again upon Jara. While doing what he said, this is what I saw.

I closed my eyes, banged my medicine drum and chanted the evocation of the All Father. The beat was fast and rapid—not my usual tempo, but I let spirit guide me.

The mists came and engulfed my room. Through the fog I could hear the cry of seagulls. Boats came into view. The Vikings were returning home; their ships laden with plunder. Folks on the jetty were cheering and preparing a great celebration for the returning warriors.

Then the vision switched to a new scene.

I was sitting in the mead hall drinking honey ale from a horn. The joyous shouts of the people swept over me and I was intoxicated with happiness. Stories of brave deeds filled the room, hecklers added jokes to the tale and happy laughter rang about. These were my people and I was grateful for the gifts the gods had bestowed on us, I wallowed in this feeling of being home.

A dark hooded figure made his way from the hall entrance door, seen by no one but me. He sat opposite upon a bench and took a swig from my horn. Then he wiped his mouth with the sleeve of his great cloak, before he pulled back his hood to reveal himself.

Odin sat before me. "I have just made a toast for the others, the nameless." His one eye pierced my thoughts.

He could tell I had no clue who "the others" were.

Quick as a flash, he swirled his cloak around me, then swooped it off again. I was thrown into the carnage of a burning settlement. There were flames, and thick black acrid smoke filled my lungs and the smell of death was in my nostrils. The screams of women, the wailing of children and cries of dying men assaulted my ears. My senses were overloaded, I just wanted to close my eyes and be back in the joy of the mead hall with my people celebrating our victory.

Odin said, "Observe, take in that which you see and always give thanks to the others. You celebrate victory. These are the defeated. You enjoy your plunder but these are the plundered. As you thank the boar for the meat he provided, take a moment to think of the vanquished and wounded. This is the other aspect of Jara."

He grabbed at a passing child, picking her up with one swoop of his arm. The girl was about ten, her hair matted with blood and two lines down her face where her tears had washed away the dirt and soot.

"Look into her face," Odin said. "This day she has lost everything, her home, her family all prospects of a good life." He released the child and she ran off into the desolation, to who knows where.

My heart was filled with shame, with pity. My people had done this and I was cheering and drinking along with all the rest. Swirling his cloak once more, Odin and I were back at the feast in the mead hall.

Now my eyes looked differently upon the celebration, the enjoyment faded for me. It felt obscene and wrong.

"Do not disrespect their sacrifice. Life is short. Enjoy each moment. There might come a day when the coin is turned and it is your village burnt to the ground, your children left orphaned and lonely. This day is yours but always give thanks to the others." He raised it high before he banged the mead horn loudly on the table.

THUMP!

I was back from my vision and pondered on the meaning of the lesson, then understood its wisdom.

Jara is also the rune of balance, work, rest and play. Just as it is the reward for effort put in, it is also the balance of good and evil, of light and dark, day and night, luck and misfortune. It is the pleasure-pain theory in practical terms. This is just pure physics; everything balances itself out in the end.

So when in the future you celebrate a great victory, give a thought for the defeated. At a wedding, raise your glass to the lonely.

JARA (yar-rah)
Mystical: Celebration after hard work
Mythical: Balance/Yin & Yang
Magical: Cycle of the year/
Cause and effect

STORY FIFTEEN:

EOH

MY VISION ON EOH DID not happen on my sacred walk. It happened somewhere else within the town. A place called Wearyall Hill. This is the site of the Holy Thorn tree that's said to be grown from Joseph of Arimathea's staff, and the place of the first Christian church in Britain. It is a site of holiness, which pilgrims from all around the world visit.

For me it is the epicenter of female Faerie energy within Avalon, which is something that I've found very difficult to understand. Just as I have worked with Gwynn Ap Nudd (the Celtic Faerie King), I must work with or at least understand Credillad, the Celtic Faerie Queen. For me personally, Wearyall Hill is where she dwells; it is her kingdom, her throne.

In my time in Glastonbury, there were not many occasions when I practiced my medicine at that location. Most of those times I did not feel a welcoming energy. The land wights or spirits, made me feel uneasy.

It was a summer's evening and I was taking a stroll to the Tor, when a flash of light caught my eye and redirected my gaze to the site of the Holy Thorn tree. I believed this was spirit letting me know that I had a message waiting for me there. With an immediate about turn, I changed the direction of my journey and headed towards the sacred site.

The Holy Thorn tree at that time was a live tree with a few green sprigs still attached. A cascade of bright ribbons and prayers were tied to the protective railings at its base. Since then, it has been cut down or murdered by unknown parties but that is another story. I gave offerings and said prayers but for me this was not the site of my magic.

I strolled higher up the hill; let my mind focus on the fibers of the web that guides us all. In the semi-trance walk of the shaman, I read the aura of this venue. I came to a dead stop at an anthill that faced back to the Tor. At this time of day, the Tor glowed like an emerald green castle in the setting sun, unmasking its magic for everyone to see. Part of me wished I had taken my usual route, but then I could not observe its true majesty from there.

As before, on my previous sorties up here, the spirits here made themselves known, and a shiver ran up my spine. I sensed a presence and turned to see or feel a green ball of light, similar to the goblin spirit that had knocked me off the Tor, but far more aggressive. The energy ball rushed towards me in what I can only explain as a charge challenge, and stopped dead about four feet in front of my face. At its closest point I saw an image within the sphere of green light, a green baboon-like creature, baring his long, sharp fangs at me. The beast retreated back to the tree line, only to challenge me twice more. I did not move, I did not flinch but stuck my shaman stick in the ground in front of me, between us, to let the creature know I was not afraid. Strange as it may sound, I was not.

By now this green light had been joined by three others all of various shades of green, two darker and one lighter. The lighter energy ball was bigger than its comrades and was growing in size by the second. This sphere approached, not so much a sphere but more elongated like a leaf or a flickering green flame. As the apparition came closer the figure within came into focus.

A beautiful woman stood before me, with the perfect naked body. She was hovering six inches above the ground. She drifted closer, slowly closer. Goose bumps appeared on my skin, not from fear but from excitement. This was truly a goddess in front of me and all my protections fell away. Vulnerable and open, I allowed her to approach.

No words were spoken but her long elegant arm reached out, touched my cheek and my whole body shook. Bear in mind that this was about eight o'clock on a summer's evening. I vaguely had the recollection of a middle aged couple pass by with a Springer spaniel but at this time to me the world of man was just a shadow, a soft breeze somewhere in the distance.

The green goddess leaned forwards and kissed me. She did not kiss my lips. She kissed my soul. I had been touched by an angel and just lingered in the total rapture of the moment. Her eyes gazed deep within me. She said, "You can have it all. Just ask, my Lord."

At that moment, somewhere in the recesses of my shamanic mind, I heard another voice call.

"This is a test, to see what you will settle for." The voice of Goll faded away, or I blacked it out, I am not quite sure, as the emerald siren kissed me once again. I can only describe the feeling as being drunk and falling into a heavenly sleep.

Then a flash of clarity saved me and I knew this was a Faerie test—one to see what I was willing to sell out for. Some people like shiny things, gold and silver; some want fame and notoriety. For me the test was female affection, something I have craved since childhood. My wife Tara had been in the states for about two months and I missed her deeply. She was the source of my oxytocin! It's the hormone men can only get from the affection of their partner or bonding with a pet. I had neither, and the Faerie Queen knew it.

Her touch saturated my brain with serotonin, inducing me to a state of gaga-ness. Deep within my medicine man's soul I grabbed at some words. "I have come for wisdom and truth. That is what I seek."

The Faerie Queen released her hold on me and retreated back to her companions at the tree line. I was charge challenged by the green light once more and then the host of energies was gone. My heart was empty and tears welled in my eyes. I had passed the test but that which I longed for was gone.

I gathered myself and left this place. I would visit the Egg stone and reside in some masculine energy, before going back to my empty flat, for if I went home now, I knew I would sob like a baby. All of the endorphins she had given me were drained away by my rejection of her; any other that I may have had in reserve were completely burnt up.

Beside the Dragon Stone I sat, sobbed and called to Gwynn. Then came his answer: "I see, white bear that you have tasted my sorrow. For she is Credillad, she is my love, the Summer Queen, as I am the Winter King. I thank you, little brother, for not being seduced by her beauty. For that I will honour you with great teaching in the years ahead." Gwynn walked beside me as I left the Tor.

Upon a bench at the base of the hill, he sat beside me (at least his spirit did) and we wallowed in our loneliness for some time. Then I finally gathered my strength and left to go home. Part of me had been seduced by the Faerie Queen and always would be. Gwynn knew that, and it made our bond stronger for I had not given in to the temptation.

We are all tested at times in our lives but we must keep focus. It is only in the heat of battle or the arms of passion when we can tell if we have the metal to see it through. Keep your eye on the target, draw your bow and keep utter concentration to see it through till the end.

"Have total belief in your own abilities." That is my vision on Eoh.

EOH (ee-yohh)

Mystical: Focus

Mythical: The Archer/god Ullr

Magical: Yggdrasil (Tree of Life)

STORY SIXTEEN:

PEORTH

Wﬁ¹TH Peorth, I will explain a situation that happened in the realm of men that led to my friendship with Tim Raven. It follows the events of my opening a store in Glastonbury and how that caused conflict with others around the town.

We moved into our store and displayed our handcrafted products. Every single thing my wife and I sell has been made by us, blessed and set to its purpose for those who would be its bearer in the future. We both honestly thought we would be welcomed with open arms, as this is a town of spiritual folks, and we would be amongst our own.

What came to pass started as a misunderstanding brought about by information withheld from us.

We opened our store and happily displayed our products. Other shopkeepers visited us within our immediate area. I thought they had come to wish us well and to welcome us to the community, but no. They had come to tell us that we could not sell the things that we made. They sold similar items and that it was an unwritten rule that they never step on each other's toes when it comes to products.

They informed me that they were not happy for me to sell anything to do with Celtic or Norse culture, especially the runes. As that pretty much meant everything we made, we were a bit shocked. No one had ever mentioned this when we signed the lease on the store.

As the runes are my spiritual path and my connection to the gods this would not or could not ever happen.

I explained my predicament and said that what they'd asked was impossible. We parted ways.

Tara went straight home and checked out the lease on the premises. It stated in black and white, that the shop was allowed to sell, and be open for readings of the rune stones.

The next morning when I opened the shop someone had pushed a spell under the door...to this day I know not who did it. This was like water off a duck's back to me and I disposed of it at a certain place on the Tor, releasing its energy back into the earth.

My wife Tara took this very badly. Maybe it was meant for her, not me. She was a stranger in these lands and felt very unwelcome. Whoever sent us the message...it did not work. I was very sad that I could not have had a close and friendly relationship with others who follow the same Norse and Celtic paths. We are too few to be at odds with each other and I wish my Northern brothers and sisters well in all they do. May Odin's blessing be upon them.

Anyway, it was during this awkward situation that an interesting fellow visited my shop. He came in wearing a top hat, an ankle length black coat and carrying a pennywhistle. Smiling blue eyes shone out between his long, straw-coloured hair and the brim of his hat. He introduced himself and seemed really interested in the things I sold. This guy had a great deal of knowledge and it was good to speak to a fellow sage. We discussed our spiritual paths, my connection to the runes, the energy that I put into each of the talismans I made, but most of all my commitment to Odin and the path of truth that I walk.

We spoke for a long time, being very comfortable in each other's company. It was as if we had known each other a lifetime. I believe I had known this man in many lifetimes because he instantly felt like a brother to me, a comrade. He then revealed that he was an extremely close friend of the people who had been offended by me opening my shop. He had come in only to check me out, test out my energy and had then concluded that he knew my path was true and would try and resolve the issue with his friends. I was a bit taken aback, and then it dawned on me. I would have done exactly the same for my friends and I thanked him for his honesty.

I told Tim, "I can never not sell or read runes. They are who I am, they have saved me and led me to the arms of the gods."

I am still sad to this day that the issue over the shop was not sorted out. But that problem led me to have friendship with Tim Raven. Since that first meeting we have had many mystic encounters together and hours upon hours of spiritual talks.

The purpose of using this story is to explain that a man must use his own luck, to be proud of whom he is. In the poem "Beowulf," when a stranger enters a new village he must Peorth before the tribe: tell the story of his life and let any man challenge him. If he is true he will prevail.

Luck in not a matter of sitting back and waiting for it to come along. It is a force within you that rises up and says, "Yeah, I can do that. This is who I am." When the time is right you should grab chances with both hands.

I now know. It was luck that bought me to Glastonbury. The fates manifested the dispute and luck led to my coming together with Tim. In all of these events, Peorth was present but nothing would have manifested had I had not grabbed my chances when they arose.

PEORTH (perr-throw)

Mystical: Luck/chance

Mythical: The Cauldron

Magical: Ginnungagap (the
Void, or nothingness, where
all outcomes are possible)

STORY SEVENTEEN:

ALGIZ

MY OWN SHAMANIC EXPERIENCE GOES back to a magical tool the dwarves were making for me when I encountered the goblin on the Tor. I had visited the Egg stone several times and on each visit Gwynn informed me that my gift was nearly ready. While I was on an adventure one summer at dawn, I was told that a shaman's staff was ready and waiting.

Feeling at peace, I sat on the Dragon's Egg with one hand placed against the cold surface of the rock and the other clasping the handle of my sacred knife. The knife's blade was blade plunged into the earth so as to ground my energy and help keep me connected to complete the circuit of power.

The Faerie King's voice echoed in my ears. "It is ready boy," said Gwynn. "The smiths of the underworld have worked long and hard. The tool this land gifts you is complete. It is now here in this realm and you must open your heart and find it. Look hard and long. Open your shamanic eye and feel its presence. Let its radiance guide you the where it lies sleeping, ready to be awoken by your touch."

I did as I was told and allowed myself to wander. Drawn by the pulsing energy radiating from the Faerie wood below, I headed in that direction. I could see and feel a golden fog that lured me along the twisting path. I was not alone in my quest. A gathering of the Fae flittered around me as I went on my search. Then at the very corner of the wood, in front of a huge dense bramble bush, a golden glow swirled into a ball of buzzing light. Half in the bush, half on the path, I scanned within its light to find my prize. On the ground just off to the side, laying half hidden in some stinging nettles, was a long staff, with three prongs at the top, like an Algiz.

I picked it up and felt it in my hand. The horde of curious Fae gathered closer and closer. Their energy was suffocating. They really wanted me to accept the gift. And, at that moment, I knew it was wrong! The arms were nearly, but not quite, right. The Faeries were too eager for me to take it. I cast it back to the ground and as I did, I felt the woodland sprites groan with displeasure. Their ruse had not foiled me.

Turning, I ran back up the Tor and sat once more upon the Egg. "If there is truly a gift for me, not another bloody test, show me exactly where it is or just leave me alone. No more Faerie tricks today please."

Gwynn stood behind me. I felt his presence as he loomed over me. His magical hands rested upon my shoulders and a vision was seeded in my third eye. I saw the golden ball once again, and I saw the rejected staff, and then I saw beneath the bramble bush, a glimpse of something wonderful.

I hurtled down the Tor, rushed along the path and returned to the gathering of the Fae. I crouched down on my hands and knees and fumbled beneath the bramble. My fingers just brushed the gift, managing to push it further away. I now lay completely flat on my belly, bramble thorns pushed into my cheeks. They scratched at me like a kitten's claws, but at last I had a firm grip on it. With a huge yank I pulled it free of its hiding place.

It was not as I imagined. In my dreams it had been the size of a druid's staff, the likes of which Gandalf weals in *Lord of the Rings*. This was much shorter but the three arms at the top formed a perfect Algiz. I tried to test it as a walking stick but it came up short. For it to work in this way I had to walk like a cripple, my back all hunched. That did not feel right at all.

I left the Faerie wood and returned to thank Gwynn and the dwarves for my gift and as I walked the stick naturally found its place in the crook of my arm like a peace pipe, like a baby, like a part of me.

As I strolled back through the town with my new prize, some of the people that I passed shied away from it. Others were drawn to it, but all noticed it.

Back at the flat, I took some of Tara's deerskin and wrapped the handle, then studded it with brass rivets. It was beginning to look and feel right. My phone vibrated from where it lay on the kitchen side, letting me know a message had arrived. It was Tim asking for me to meet him for a brew. He'd had visions and we needed to talk.

I took my new toy and strolled through the town. Tim was already there with two cups of decaf tea, hot and ready. I know that is an extremely sad drink for two warrior wizards but that is what we drink! He noticed my spirit gift straight away and I told him of the morning's events.

Tim's response was, "Well done bro, passing the Faerie test, but you know you need bells on that. So you can tell the spirits that you are coming and that you are not afraid. Those that mean you harm will run from it. Those that mean you well will approach and be recognized."

"Tim, that has already happened to me," I said. "As I walked back through the town, it could tell friend from foe. Bells definitely feel right. There will be nine of them. One for each realm. The spirits in all the nine worlds will know I'm coming."

People in the town came to recognize me by the shaman's stick and the spirits on the Tor could hear me coming even on the darkest night. The stick became my number one tool for taking me on visions, and it still is. Goll's caribou has bells on his halter and as I close my eyes and rattle my stick, I feel them approach.

It has protected me in many an encounter with dark energy and it is always present when holding a healing session. One winter solstice, it snowed heavily and the temperature dropped well below freezing. I had been up working my medicine at the Egg stone since two a.m. It was now approaching five a.m. and I began to struggle my way back down through the heavy drifts.

It had been a crystal clear night and dawn was at least three hours away. The frigid air clung to my breath as the dragon's mist accompanied every exhalation. Below, I heard the bang of the bottom gate, and a lone figure approached up the path. I wasn't sure whether it was spirit, man, friend or foe, so I slowed my pace and rattled the bells on the Algiz stick.

Tim's voice echoed through the still night air. "Fucking hell, that's either Father Christmas or you, bro! How long you been up 'ere?"

"Since about two. I was just heading down."

"Fancy coming back to the Egg with me do some *work*?"

"Course I do."

We both headed back along the slippery and winding path.

As we walked, Tim pointed something out to me. "This is winter solstice, the most important time for the Tor, and it is right now that the doorway is open. All those so-called men and women who follow the path and wear the fancy gowns? Where the fuck are they now? I could have bet my life on you being up here, bro. They will turn up when it's light, bang a few drums sing a few songs. This is when the real medicine is done. This is where the real shamans are."

"I know, bro. I have to do this. It is for me to honour my gods. I don't give a fuck if anyone sees me or not, as long as spirit sees me."

We continued with spirit work until the dawn broke over the ancient Tor and the throng of worshipers made their way up to the top. Tim joined his Celtic brothers. He is highly respected within the Druid circles and I stood to the side and away from the majority of the people, stuck my Algiz stick in the ground, and chanted my sacred chants as the New Year, after winter solstice, was born.

To most people of this gathering, I was an outsider, an evil Anglo-Saxon, who worshiped the Norse gods. How dare I step foot on their Holy Celtic place! That was to be my role in Glastonbury for the duration of my stay in Avalon. To me it did not matter because the spirits of the Tor embraced me and recognized my path of truth. The Algiz stick kept these people wondering.

Find that which protects you and hold it close and near at all times. That source of protection stems for the love you have for yourself, which will not allow you to put yourself in harm's way.

That power is always with you.

As the *Havamal* instructs: "When travelling on the open road never sleep far from your sword and spear."

ALGIZ (alll-geez)

Mystical: Self love/Protection

Mythical: The Sacred Elk/Stag

Magical: Divine Male and Female

STORY EIGHTEEN:

SOWELO

MY EXPERIENCES WITH SOWELO TESTED my belief structure, eventually stripping it away and building it back together with a greater strength than ever before.

My place in Glastonbury, seeded by this rune stone, was an old shaggy bramble bush. Even before I cast my rune at this place, it was a healing shrine to me. I would go there, touch the leaves and thorns, and feel total love and belonging.

My first encounter with this holy bush was on a damp spring morning. I had been taking a shamanic walk focusing on the energies and auras of the local plants, talking to and receiving wisdom from a variety of trees and shrubs. As I approached this place in my semi-trance, I could sense a heat begin to warm my cold bones.

I stood before the bramble and touched one of its leaves, using care to close my hand around it. As my fingers shut, a golden thread of light came out from the plant, wrapping its cord like a vine around my wrist. I allowed the plant being to pull my shaman spirit from my body and lead me gently through a gateway at its roots and into to a vast cavern beneath the Tor.

When this happened, it was in a time of immense loneliness for me. Tara had been gone over three months. It always seems when at my lowest ebb the medicine of the runes comes to heal.

The enchanted cave I was ushered into by the plant's energy recharged my spirit. I felt honoured to have received such a gift.

This cave had a regal majesty; it gave me a sense that kings dwelt there. I returned back to my body. Every day from that point on, the bramble became part of my spirit walk. It always said a hello and gave thanks when I passed it. It was no great surprise to me when the rune I picked from my pocket to leave at this spot was Sowelo.

It was early summer and I had just come back from a vision with Goll. Within the journey a rune had been cast, it was of course Sowelo. "Go to your place of the Sun. There is someone who wants to meet you. Keep your eyes and your heart open, remember what you see, every detail will be important." Goll then waved me on my way and continued picking his teeth with a twig.

I knew exactly what and where he meant and so I made my way to the bush.

I greeted this holy bramble with a bowed head and gave thanks for his companionship. I held out both my hands to cradle a cluster of its barbs. As my fingers touched the leaves, the whole plant burst into a brilliant glow, as if it was on fire. Through the glare and dazzle of the bright light I could see a figure standing behind and above the bush, maybe twenty feet away. The blaze of light faded away to a soft glow revealing a radiant man, dressed in a white cloak with long blonde hair. He was silhouetted by the outline of the Tor.

My knees went weak and I dropped to the ground. I knew I was standing in the presence of Christ. This rocked me to my core. Had all my teachings and runic knowledge led me to the Christian Master to start again? This figure of Jesus...(as an aside, it feels nuts to be naming him, to be writing this as I saw it in this vision)...raised the sleeves of his cloak to reveal a rune on each forearm. Algiz was on his left and Ur was on his right. (This is the reason I have those runes tattooed on me in those exact locations.) They are the marks of a healer: to give with the right hand or side, and to take away with the left. The sword and the shield—in one.

He spoke into my heart with soft words. "It is all the same. Medicine, paths, gods. Just have faith in yours." Slowly he picked up a shield from beside his feet, revealing the sun wheel of the rune Baldr embossed upon the front. "Christ and Baldr are one." The revelation hit me like a lightning bolt and what dawned on me was that this was totally obvious.

Then Christ was gone and the glow of the bush faded. I was left awestruck and shaking on the side of the Tor.

I heard a voice beside me speak: "Goodbye my friend. We all have our time, so don't waste yours."

It was the bramble bush.

Not quite sure what this meant, and still distilling the previous events, I thanked him and left to return home. The rest of that day went by in a flash. I was floating. The Christ light had appeared during two of my healings with clients. It seemed I had learnt how to tune into his vibration. Later in the day, I tried to get hold of Tim but he was out of town so I decided to go back to the bramble the following morning, sit beneath it and journey to council with Goll.

The crows were calling, louder than ever, as I rose the next dawn. When I got to the place of Sowelo, the bush was gone. All that remained in that spot was a pile of ash and a couple of charred branches. (One of which sits beside me as I'm writing this book and is now at every reading I hold.) I sat beside the charred earth, immersed my hands deep in the ash and cried like a baby.

The golden light was gone, the healing glow blown out. The holy bush's last act was to connect me to and help me understand the Christ. I wished my brother farewell and knew he would come again when the time was right. As I mentioned, I took a piece of the plant's remains and said a prayer in offering. At that moment I understood that every plant every animal that dwells on the Tor is sacred to someone or other.

Some of you may be wondering: How a bush can just burn down overnight? But from that place, I followed a path of destruction that had taken place at the same time around the base of the Tor. Sacred groves where people had left prayers and wishes, tied ribbons to trees or given crystals to the land to honour the dead–had all been destroyed. Officials of the organization, the entity that 'owns' the Tor, feel they have the right to clear away any old pagan shit they see. Even worse, they hire contractors who don't give a fuck about people's hopes and dreams, to clear and burn these holy places where we honour the land, our ancestors and loved ones, make our prayers and give our thanks. Such destruction alters what has become sacred through many human hours of prayer and vision, places that are dedicated to the old gods and the new (I mean the pagan gods of our ancestors and the rising of the goddess in this new millennia.)

How would they feel if I burned down a church because I thought it was crap; rubbish obstructing my way? Fuck, I bet they don't even lose a moment's sleep in destroying what shows up around the Tor. We who leave our marks with stones, ribbons and crystals are just fucking heathen trash to them. All I know is that I have felt more connected to god in the forest and on top of the Tor than I ever did in a church.

Anyway, that is how my sacred bramble brother met his doom and he knew it was going to happen. He knew his time was done. In conclusion to this vision about Sowelo, we all have our moment in the sun, so don't waste if. If spirit calls you embrace that moment, do it, for it may not call again. As for those people who have passed, let the warmth of their memory comfort you on the cold nights ahead. Let grief go; be free of grief but allow the memories to bring joy.

I now know the power of Sowelo, Christ, Baldr, the bramble. All have that golden light that is all healing and I have been blessed by it.

SOWELO [so-we-low]

Mystical: Joy and wonderment

Mythical: The god Baldr [sun god]

Magical: The Path of the Dragon

STORY NINETEEN:

TIRWAZ

I<small>T WAS</small> N<small>OVEMBER AND THE</small> sky went dark by about five p.m. It had been a busy day at work and I had just decided to have lamb chops, mash and peas for my supper. As I made my way to Morrison's in search of mint sauce and of course, the chops (I know to some of you out there reading this book will think: 'mint sauce and meat...what the hell?'...but these are the foods of the gods to an Englishman) the voice of Odin boomed in my head. "In this night, boy, much is to be learned in the darkness. Journey to the Tor, the very top and await my wisdom."

My mouth was salivating at the thought of juicy chops but they (plus the mash and peas) would have to wait. I returned to my flat to grab my shaman stick and some berries as offerings. I put on my medicine hat (the one with the blue feather) and set off up the winding path to St. Michael's tower at the top of the Tor.

I passed a few unsuspecting tourists on the way down through the darkness. The look on their faces showed disdain, as first they heard the bells, then saw this nut in a top hat come into view. The vision of me always scared the crap out of them, as it should, for the Tor is no place to be for the uninitiated after dark, especially on a night as dark as this. I stopped and sat on a rock to make sure they were well clear before I moved on.

At the summit, a strong brisk wind caught me as I left the lee-ward side of the tower. I scattered my offerings on the ground and stood in the position of Algiz to say my prayers and await Odin's teachings.

What came instead were dread, terror and fear. The black night was moving around me, swirling around me, as the shades moved closer. Shades are the shadow beings that dwell in the dark. They are the ghosts that haunt your dreams, they are the sources of that feeling you get when the hairs on the back of your neck go up and you don't know why. There can be no angels if there are no demons, and at night, this is their place of residence and I was an intruder. They wanted me gone or dead and they had no preference either way.

I had encountered the shades before and seen one so close up I could taste its breath. It is only when they are within a foot of your face that you can get a brief glimpse of their evil snarling features, their dark muddy green eyes glaring at you.

This night there was a horde of them and they wanted my blood, my soul, my sanity. There are times on all the paths of all shamans, paths when madness could take over. Tonight my fear was so strong that the thin cord that keeps me grounded was at a breaking point and I could have been devoured by the world of darkness.

They began by tugging at me, this way then that. I was pushed further and further back, finally pinned against the wall of the tower. My heart pounded in my chest, my knees weakened and as I was struck across the side of the head. I fell on all fours.

Anyone who says ghosts and demons don't exist may as well say that the night is an illusion. If there is day there must be night. If there is good there must be evil. Evil itself is subjective depending on what side of the fence you are standing at the time. All I know is that these fuckers live on the other side of the fence to me. I felt real pain as I was kicked in the guts.

The attack became a blur and I awaited the long ship to take me to the afterlife. But instead Odin appeared and spoke in my mind. "You are most powerful at dawn as the day rises. As the sun comes up, so does your strength. Your enemy will never attack you then, they only attack when you are weakest. So call on your blood, call on your bones, call on your courage and stand once more. Call on Tirwaz and make not one more step back in retreat. Call your guides to the shield wall and stand strong."

I started to chant, and from my churning stomach the sound arose, finally exiting my throat in a deep, earthy groan as the words echoed in the dark, the shades stopped dead in their tracks. I rose to my feet. Somewhere I found enough energy and lashed out my shaman stick. Now I was screaming my Galdr and claiming my space. Like an erupting volcano the words spewed out. I drove them off me and down, away from the tower.

I was angry, not just with them but with myself for being so pathetic. I made a good size clearing in their masses; I stumbled away from the tower and began down the steep steps that led back away from the Tor. My legs felt like lead. I had to drag each one and flick it forwards to move, but I did it. I would not give in.

Halfway down, the shades charged at me again, calling on their own powers for this was their sacred place and they needed to defend it. Swearing and screaming like a banshee, I smashed and struck in all directions. My enemy was driven off once more. The further down the path, the weaker their strength and the lesser their numbers, for I knew that as I fear the dark, they fear the light, and now only the bravest of them stalked me. By the time I reached the first field at the bottom, I knew that they would not advance beyond the safety of the gate and I screamed back at them with the top of my voice. "Is that all you've got you fucking shade cunts! Fucking look at me I am still fucking alive."

I was so charged up, the mead of victory flooded my veins and I could have taken on an army.

As I passed through the gateway back onto the road to town, and while standing completely still, I came upon an old man and woman with a Yorkshire terrier.

"Evening," I said as they passed by.

Strange—they didn't reply. Perfectly normal event to see the Mad Hatter screaming like a lunatic and fighting with ghosts?

Many of my shamanic adventures cross paths with dog walkers for it is in the peace and solitude of the Tor that shamans go for wisdom and the dog brigades go there to unwind from the day's stress.

Back at the flat, I collapsed on the couch and flicked on the TV. It was late now and I had missed my favourite shows, but far worse than that, I had missed my lamb chops. So my victory feast was a pot noodle instead, not just any pot noodle but a chicken and mushroom King Pot that I devoured like a hungry wolf.

Tirwaz is the rune to call on when all else has failed. Better to go down fighting than to be slaughtered like a dog. This rune can summon up a giant inside you, if your path is just and your cause is true. Victory is never easy but the glow of old glory can keep you warm on a very cold night.

As I was writing this chapter, a client emailed me about her brother. He had been haunted or taunted by a demon that attached itself to him. I made a sigil for him, which will allow him to call on Tirwaz to defeat his demon. He must take some of the responsibility himself and claim his space. The talisman will take on the form of a helm, designed like a shield, and it calls on and combines different runic energies.

My work often involves dealing with demons and attachments. For some of the light workers I know, my path is too hard-core, too extreme, but for me that is the way it has to be. I am a warrior and not afraid to go into the dark places, for Odin walks beside me.

TYR (tir-waz)

Mystical: Victory

Mythical: The god Tyr/Discipline

Magical: The spine/The

core of your values

STORY TWENTY:

BERKANA

Now for how Berkana. When it came into my life, it changed the way I saw the world. It would make sense to say that this rune was the first I dropped on my walk of Glastonbury but that is not true; it was the second. It took a long time for the teachings of this rune to show itself.

I had connected to its energy and worked with the lessons and chants of this symbol, especially with my female clients, but it was always Freyja's presence that overrode the situations I experienced in vision. Female energy! I had not learned the lessons of the maid, so how could I understand the lessons of the mother?

Within the mystical worlds of psychics and healers and shamans, there is the ever-present shadow of enchantment. This is when female healers get male clients enchanted by them. Male healers find that some women become obsessed by them. This for me is always Freyja's energy. The client can't help himself or herself for they have found someone they can be openly spiritual with, someone who listens, understands and can help. Never ever should this be abused, for it is a sacred test from spirit.

So it seemed to me whilst I was working in Glastonbury I was continually locked in the energy of Fehu and the lessons of Freyja. Not until I came to the United States, where I had few clients, did I lock myself away in my healing room and allow the true teachings of Frigga, or Berkana, to come to me.

Summer solstice 2013 was an extremely low point for me. I wanted, I yearned, I longed, to be back on the Tor, chanting my prayers as the sun rose. Instead I sat in my lonely healing room in Washington state, closed my eyes, shook my shaman stick and heard the caribou trotting his way to me through the cosmic mists. This was one of the very few times that Goll appeared to me here in America.

This time I was not at the council fire but at the top of the hill above Bushy Combe farm in Glastonbury. At this place several years before, a ghostly woman had passed me by as the dawn broke. Our eyes connected, we smiled and passed. Turning to take one more glance at her, she was gone, into the mists, or was never really there. Here I was again at the same spot in the same mists, with Goll. He was perched on his reindeer and held the rune Berkana in his grubby hand.

He sniffed and wiped a dewdrop from the end of his nose with his wrinkled sleeve. I noticed that Goll was more disheveled than usual as he spoke, "Just look at the rune and focus, for you boy are easily distracted by things that are too ugly to face."

No sooner had the image of the rune triggered these thoughts in my mind, the shaman vanished and was replaced by a sound. It was a haunting, beautiful sound. The chanting of young women filled my ears, my heart and my soul. I had heard this before and it usually protected me when I was on vision. I knew when to call them.

These girls were the handmaidens of Avalon. How I originally connected with them is another story for another book. Now they were approaching me out of the mists. One-by-one they came, nine in total. Whether this has any relevance to the nine worlds of Odin I have no idea but there is always nine of them.

Dressed in flowing, white chiffon gowns with daisies in their hair, they floated across the ground and around me.

Three were blonde, three were dark haired and three had locks the colour of copper. They circled me once then formed an avenue, like guards of honour. They now stood still while chanting their intoxicating song.

Let me digress here and give more information about these women: These were the maidens of legend, who led the fallen kings of Britain to Albion, to dwell and rest beneath the Tor waiting a time when they would be needed again. Among those who the sisters carried across the lake to Avalon was the mighty and holy Arthur, whose body sleeps within the mound. Arthur is known in legend to be "The once and future king of Britain."

I sat completely still just listening to their magical voices, and it sent me into a trance within a trance. Then she came, taller than the others, gathered and out of the fog she appeared. Frigga, as I had never seen her before, shining, radiant and glowing like the morning sun.

I have had a certain gift since childhood: I could tell as soon as a woman was pregnant because I can see a glow. This was the same pulsing glow of the mother figure standing before me now.

She came closer and closer. I rose to greet her. My bones felt weary and they creaked. My back would not straighten. The vision in my left eye was gone and my hands were beaten and knarled as I pulled on my shaman stick in order to stand.

I was Odin!

The woman who approached was my wife. I was father, she was mother. When we caressed, a beam of light shot up into the air. It felt like the power of creation, the seed of life itself, a fusing of two souls. I was old; she was in her beautiful prime, a woman in her late thirties, early forties. My wrinkled skin, grey straggly hair and scar socket where an eye should have been, appeared beautiful to her.

Frigga kissed me on the cheek and whispered in my ear. "Your words are beautiful. Your guidance is beautiful. Your wisdom is beautiful. I love you because we have walked the road together. I am yours and you are mine, husband." She then looked deep into my one eye, with a look that of reminded me of the first time I saw my wife Tara.

Then she left slowly, turning with elegance as she revealed a sacred helm tattooed on her back. The helm! This was a magic for me to remember—the teachings of how to connect to this wonderful energy. She retreated back into the fog, escorted by the still chanting maidens. I returned from my vision within a vision, left the form of Odin behind and was myself once more in the first vision.

Goll sat beside me. He said, "That is how Odin feels for his bride, how he feels for the mother of his children. You can't get that from a quick roll in the hay. That is a love forged by time and experiences shared. It is so different to the enchantments of Freyja, but let us not put those down as not everybody gets to feel this sort of love." Goll mounted the caribou and jingled off down the path and I returned to my healing room. In Washougal. In Washington. In the United States of America.

I was overwhelmed by the power of that vision. A realization dawned on me that when I yearn for the magic, and healing for my home, a new depth comes to my teachings. I was enchanted by Glastonbury and whilst I was lost in the spell, I could not connect with the Mother's love.

Now I have.

For within Berkana's caress there is no age, no ugliness, no judgment just pure healing and all encompassing LOVE.

BERKANA (ber-kar-nah)
Mystical: Birth/New beginnings
Mythical: goddess Frigga/The Mother
Magical: The Earth/Human
Flesh/The Female Dragon

STORY TWENTY-ONE:

EHWAZ

T HIS VISION AND EVENT HAS reoccurred many times in my life. It has to do with horses. Odin's black stallion Sleipnir has visited me often, sometimes with his master upon, sometimes not, but always, great wisdom is gained.

Sleipner is not part of this particular story. This is the story about my connection to the moon stallion. It was he who guided me to Glastonbury, many, many years before I actually got there.

He first appeared when I was about 16 years old and led to an episode of me believing that I was a werewolf! That is another story, though, and it's about understanding and controlling shape-shifting.

When the moon stallion showed up, he awakened something in me that led to lucid dreams, premonitions and experiences with ghosts. I know now that this horse showed me how to see between the veils that hide us from the other dimensions. My father admitted that he had also seen this ghostly horse but he does not speak of it. In the John Wayne, macho world of my father there is no place for visions. Now that my father is older, he allows me to share and is interested in my shamanic wisdom.

At the time I first saw this stallion, I lived with my family in a pub in the Cotswolds called the Tite Inn, which had an ancient Saxon well in the cellar. Before the horse showed up for me, all was quiet. Afterwards, strange things started happening in the pub. Our guard dogs started whimpering in the night as if they were terrified. One morning we woke up to find all the furniture was stacked up against the furthest wall of the bar and the dogs were huddled in the corner quivering.

As for me, I woke in the night to find a woman with red hair standing at the end of my bed. She said, "The horse comes to take you on a journey. It may not be the journey you want to go on but it will keep coming back until you get the idea."

Anyway, let me digress.

My father was and still is a great horseman and we owned several at this time, including a magnificent Palomino stallion named Regency Cream Boy II. Creamy for short. This horse was my father's pride and joy.

On a cold and frosty moonlit evening my father looked out of the upstairs window and over the fields that adjoined our pub. He saw what he thought was Creamy still standing in the field. He shouted down the stairs at me.

"You've left my fucking horse out in the freezing cold. Go and get him in now, you useless article!"

I ran upstairs, saying, "Dad I already fed him and he is in the stable."

"Well who's that in the field? A fucking ghost?"

We both stared out the window at the silver horse, then left the warmth of the house to go outside for him to witness his stallion safely tucked up in bed. After that we went to the paddock to find out who had put their horse in our field.

We found the field completely empty.

"I must be imaging things," my father said. "I saw it too, dad."

"No you didn't, boy. Anyway I got work to do."

And that was the end of that. Not to be spoken about for another 35 years.

Have you ever wondered why bad dreams are called nightmares? This mare of the night will take you on a wild ride. In the Celtic tradition, these horrific experiences are a natural part of your initiations and an important source of wisdom and magic.

The moon stallion showed up again for me in 2003. I was already on this path and reading books on Druid and pagan traditions. Even though I lived a very materialistic lifestyle, something of the earth was calling me, something real, not plastic and fake.

It was about two a.m. I had got up to have a wee and just settled back into bed, when the vision horse appeared. The dappled grey stallion was togged out in all sorts of finery, ribbons, and bells, and his mane was plaited with pink and purple cords. A medieval saddle of fine-tooled black leather sat upon his back.

In my dream, I got on up on him, ready for a ride. I now know it was an out-of-body experience and that my soul actually left my sleeping self behind and went on an adventure.

In the vision dream, it was a fine spring day and the blossoms were on the trees as I trotted around a town on the fine stallion. I did not know the place I was in, but it echoed familiarity. I felt like the Lord Mayor as the strange colourful people by the roadside waved at me and cheered. I spurred the steed on up the main street, turning right at the top of the hill, like I knew exactly where to go.

A man wearing antlers on his head and dressed completely in ragged skins directed me left off the street and up a steep slope through a short avenue of bushes. I lowered myself flat to the horse's neck as he was a tall beast and I would have caught my face on the thorns above.

At the end of the avenue it opened out into a field, a pleasant meadow where yet more people were gathered. Music played and children danced around a maypole. They all turned to greet me as I arrived. A young lad dressed very similarly to me grabbed the stallion's bridle and I dismounted.

The people now lined the path up the field to a gateway, through which led to a steep hill with a tower upon it. As I climbed the steep path, I threw off my waistcoat, rolled up my sleeves, tightened my belt and prepared for a fight. The top was now in sight. There they were, waiting for me: three scary looking blokes all stripped to the waist, their hands were wrapped in blood stained bandages. They stood around a pole that had a hat balanced upon it.

There was no introduction or foreplay; the first man came at me, smacking me right in the mouth. I hit the deck like a sack of shit, then sat up, dazed. The three of them laughed and taunted me.

I heard, "All this effort for fuck all. All these people watching. Get up, you burk." It was not the voices of the men but the voice of my father. My dad was a good boxer and started taking me to a box-ing gym when I was about 13. I would always fight harder because I didn't want to let him down. Right here in this mad dream, I was showing him up, shaming him.

I got back to my feet and steamed straight in. Straight left, right to the body, right to the body, left jab, crushing right hook.

The first of my challenges hit the ground cold. No sooner had the dust settled then I was rushed by the second. His head and shoulders hit me hard in the guts and we both bundled over. We rolled and scuf-fled. Using my legs as much as my arms, I pinned him to the ground and held his face still with my left hand while I smashed down heavy pile driver blows with my right. I continued until his wriggling stopped, until I was kicked in the side of the face by the last of my foes.

Everything was in slow motion, as my brain struggled to gain com-plete control. A thick forearm was now pressed hard against my throat, crushing my windpipe. I reached my arms as far behind my head as I could get, then I grabbed and gouged whatever part of him I could get my fingers on. One hand full of hair and an ear, the other, one finger up his nose another in his eye. I ripped him with all my might.

There was a high-pitched squeal as he released his vise like grip from my throat and rolled away, nursing his bleeding face. I stamped on his neck from behind, once, twice. That was enough. He was done.

Panting like a dog on a boiling hot day, I walked to the pole, took off the top hat and placed it on my head. I cleared my bruised throat, spat a mouthful of blood, phlegm and half a tooth onto the ground and stamped it into the earth with my boot. I was claiming this soil as mine. Then I ran all the way down to the meadow at the bottom of the hill.

I was totally elated. The happy, joyous folks slapped me on the back with praise. As I went to mount the horse once more, a strong hand grabbed my shoulder. It was my father.

"My turn, Jeb. I may be old but this dog's still got a bite."

I stood back as my father spurred and the stallion galloped up the hill. As I watched him charge away, I woke from my dream.

Back in the world of materialism and having to make money, I went about my life.

This crazy dream haunted me continuously, until the day when I realized the town was Glastonbury, the hill the Tor. The hat is my top hat I wear now (even though it was gifted to me by the spirit of a mountain in America, but that's another story). The battle at the top was my life and death struggle with the shades and when I was down and out, the voice of the All Father egged me on and gave me the strength to continue the fight, just as my own father had done in the earlier vision. The placing of the hat upon my head symbolized the acceptance of my medicine path.

Ehwaz is the vehicle with which you make progress on your journey. You may not always like what you see or encounter but it is essential to your evolution. The spirit horse always shows me things that eventually come to pass but my responsibility is to pay attention to, decipher and learn from the message.

One last very important point: The first rune that was placed in the meadow (the meadow of the horse), the very first rune I lost, was Ehwaz. It is in that place where I give thanks to the moon stallion for guiding me true. I know he showed me, in a vision, things that would come to pass.

EHWAZ (ay-waz)
Mystical: Partnership/Progress
Mythical: The Horse/Sleipnir
Magical: The Dragon's heart

STORY TWENTY-TWO:

MANNAZ

MY VISION EXPERIENCE WITH MANNAZ helped me understand where I came from and why I must do what I do in this lifetime.

Many a morning I had walked past my place of Mannaz and felt someone watching me from far away in the distance, from a place called Butleigh Woods. The trees of this forest can be seen following the horizon from this viewpoint on the Tor.

Sometimes I could just see a glimpse of his face in my mind's eye, but no sooner it was there than it was gone. He was always challenging me as if saying, "I am the shaman of this place. Be gone, stranger."

Not long ago, I visited Stonehenge. It was packed with Asian tourists taking shots of every single blade of grass. Luckily I can block all that shit out and focus on my spiritual connection. It is such a shame that the visitors don't just put down their cameras and ask the stones what they need to see, what they need to experience. Unfortunately we live in the age of Facebook and Instagram, where every moment of our existence must be posted for others to see.

When I was a boy, I could play and climb on these stones. Now that is impossible. There are still many sacred stone sites where you can walk up to touch and commune with the stone beings, but most are unknown to travelers who fail to research.

I am lucky to be able to block out that interference and focus on my messages from the stones.

On another visit to Stonehenge, I was drawn to the corner of the site where there is an unexciting burial mound. As I tuned in, I saw another shaman standing on top, chanting to a gathered assembly of ancient people. Tara, who was behind me said that she had just had a vision, and it is not very often that she even shares them with me. When she does, they are always bang on the money. She swore she saw me standing on the mound chanting. She had no doubt it was me because I was shaking my Algiz shaman stick.

So was what I saw an echo of myself? Usually, if Tara has felt or seen something at the same time as me, I have to tell first. For her it is the only way she can believe and that is good for me. She keeps me grounded and confirms some of my own experiences.

Back to my place of Mannaz on the Tor, and to a dream I'd had before I planned to vision at this particular spot. I pulled the Mannaz rune from my pouch, sat on the ground and slowly dug my sacred blade into the earth. This action is exceptionally good at helping me recall past events. I believe the land has a far better memory than people and if you can tune in and ask it the right way, information can be downloaded to you.

I chanted. I prayed and the mists formed and carried me through time, back and away from this reality.

I was approaching a long tent covered in skins and pelts. A wolf's head hung over the door to decorate or mark the entrance. I could hear mumbled voices, men talking, and the faint crackle of a fire. I ventured nearer and peered through a gap in the wall, where two skins met. Maybe two dozen or more warriors of many ages were present all focusing on a crooked man huddled over a pile of twigs, bones and runes arranged on the floor.

The sage stopped his work and turned to face me. His sun-leathered, wrinkled face was staring right into mine. Rotten teeth, a broken nose and several scars could not mask the fact that he was I! I was him, but in another time. When it came to good looks he'd gotten the shit end of the stick. I knew he could feel me looking into the tent from outside.

He sat up and cleared away his magical tools with one sweep of his arm. The wizard then spoke in a deep, croaky voice. "Enter, strange one. Do not fear. They cannot see you; they cannot hear you. Only us who have the magic eye can see this. Why do you haunt me? Stay in your own realm."

I spoke as I walked through a gap in the wall. "I need to know who you are." I understood that he knew the question before I asked it.

"Need to know your clan, your tribe, your people? We are your people, we of the wolf clan. In your time, they are scattered to the wind like dandelion seeds. So search, find them and unite them once more, as many as you can in the precious time you have left. For I am A..... H...... descended from the Lords of Avalach, land guardian of the sacred Tor. Healer to some, oracle to others, shaman of my people and blood kin to Wotan and...you are I! Me from the distant future!"

He snatched up a hand full of dried earth and dust from the ground and cast it in my face.

"Be gone, back to your own world!" he shouted.

I thought, "You horrible fucker!" as I watched him explain to the warriors that he'd seen a spirit demon and had driven it away.

I returned to my body on the Tor remembering everything I saw and heard. Now whenever I pass this place, I remember who I was, and who I am. When I visit a new site of sacred energy, a forest, a mountain, a waterfall, I stand in the position of Mannaz and shout out loud: "I am A..... H......, descended from the Lords of Avalach, land guardian of the sacred Tor. Healer to some, oracle to others and blood kin to Odin." (Not Wotan, for in my prayers he is always called Odin. Wotan was the Saxon name for him.)

Through the rune of Mannaz I found out who I am now, who I was then, and my purpose in the world of men. I can never reveal my shamanic name...dark energy can use that as a gateway to this realm and the secret is what makes it magic.

Now I know I have to gather the lost members of my tribe. The problem is that I don't think they want to be found, especially the ones in the United States of America.

MANNAZ (mannnn-azzz)
Mystical: Mankind/Helper/Destiny
Mythical: The Hooded Man
Magical: The Anointed Priest

STORY TWENTY-THREE:

LAGUZ

T HIS CHAPTER INVOLVES TWO SHORT experiences. The first was an encounter with Laguz in the realm of men. The second, a message Odin gave me while I was in a shamanic trance.

It was time to celebrate Imbolc. Imbolc is a pagan festival that celebrates the returning of the sun after the winter darkness—the turning of the year from Crone back to Maid as spring is born. I had been up on the Tor during the dark hours.

I'd said my prayers and gave offerings as the dawn broke. As I left the Tor, I passed the White Spring, which is very important on this day, and a crowd had gathered to hold ceremony within the Well House Cave. I thought, "If Tim is there, I will wish him well and maybe I'll stay for the blessing."

I went inside and it didn't feel right at all. I get these sudden urges and always go with them. I thought "Fuck this for a game of soldiers! I'm off."

As I was leaving through the entrance, I bumped into Tim who had just arrived. I told him of my concerns and we both decided to go consult the spirits at a certain sacred place within the cave. We took up our positions in Hern's Corner, a shrine honouring the horned god of the forest. "We should keep an eye out here, bro. See what these fuckers are up to?" Tim was as wary as me. He stood in the far right corner and I seated myself in the left, with my back against the wall.

The folks who had gathered consisted of all sorts, from old men to toddlers and there were probably half a dozen dogs scattered within the group. The organizers said their bit, drums were banged and the doors were shut. To come from utter darkness and celebrate the return of the light is the nature of this ceremony. Then every single candle was blown out.

As the last red glow of my candle's wick died, I felt it enter. The hairs on the back of my neck prickled and I took on the shape of the white bear. I sensed extreme protection was needed. The entity I was feeling made its way amongst us. A slimy black serpent had been called from up the depths. It slithered a path between these unsuspecting people. It approached the corners where Tim and I were positioned and I growled, deep and powerful, letting it know I'd seen it. Its eyes switched back and forth from me to Tim, then it flicked out its tongue and tasted our scent. The creature retreated back into the darkness.

In the utter blackness, dogs whimpered, children cried, the crowd became uneasy and shuffled around. I had an uncontrollable urge to smash down the doors and let light drive the evil away. Then the first candle was relit, then another, then another and light returned once more. Finally the huge wooden door was opened. Whatever had stalked us had returned to its lair. I turned to Tim and I knew he had felt it also.

"Did you feel that, bro?" he asked.

"Fucking right I did, Tim. I just sat here in white bear growling at the fucking thing."

"I don't know about you, bro but I was close to doing a Ned Flanders impersonation by screaming and running out the door."

I laughed. Tim had the knack of explaining an exact sensation.

"Yeah that was it, bang on! I was shitting myself."

Back outside in the light, we scanned the crowd to see if we could feel who was behind this, but they were hidden. To this day I have not been in the White Spring since and will not go there until I see it has returned to purity. I feel it has been corrupted. Tim reckoned it was something to do with the dark guardians, but this is his area of expertise and I will leave well alone. It is very important to understand what you have the right to get involved with and what you don't. I know to not stick my hooter in where it is not wanted;

especially if I don't understand what the fuck I am sticking it into. Watch, learn...say nothing until things become clear. This is a message I learned from Odin very early on and it had served me well.

When I return to Glastonbury, I will make a special visit to the White Spring to see what I feel, to see if the energy has changed. I wrote this tale because water represents emotion and the emotion that reared its head here was fear. An almost uncontrollable fear in the form of a black snake.

It only takes a drop of something dark to taint something pure. If fear is allowed to rise it can defeat the mightiest warrior.

On the other hand, a small flame of light can make sense out of much darkness. A small amount of light can erase a large amount of dark fear.

The second tale is based on a purely spiritual experience.

I was led to my place of Laguz by Odin, who showed himself at my council fire. He beckoned for me to follow him and I ran behind as he rode the mighty Sleipnir (Odin's eight-legged horse) across the Tor. As in all my visions, my place of Laguz appears as a waterfall, and there it was, in the distance.

I heard him first, then saw Tim sitting on a rock playing his pennywhistle. He waved as Odin and I approached. The All Father clapped his hands and a giggling group of young maidens or sirens ran to grab Tim and me by the hands. They led us into the falling, crashing waters.

Odin said, "Enjoy the fountain of youth, then return to me refreshed and washed clean." He left us in the water.

The maidens all stripped naked and undressed the two of us. We plunged beneath the spectacular falls of turquoise and white. The golden light of the sun cascaded through the clear waters, and dappled the wall of rock behind the fall. We were being pampered by these angels. I felt like a god.

I watched Tim's face being scrubbed by a maiden with handful of oak leaves. Once the maiden had finished her task and moved her hand away, instead of Tim looking younger, he looked older, a fucking lot older. I stared down at own my hands—my wrinkled, knarled and crooked hands.

"Fuck me, bro, you look fucking ancient!" Tim pointed at me. He was laughing.

"Don't laugh too much...you don't look that great, either," I replied, feeling that we had both been fooled by a Faerie trick and had failed Odin's test. I was sure the Fae would show themselves, as they love nothing better to gloat when one of their pranks has succeeded.

Outside in the cold air it was Odin who waited, not faeries. He threw us both a cloak of deep midnight blue (as near black as blue can get) the exact same colour as his own cloak. "Do you understand the lesson?"

"Yes, we were tricked thinking we could grow young again."

"No stupid boy!" Odin snapped back at me. "This is no trick. That is the fountain of youth, the place where you leave youth behind. Leave the distractions of beauty, vanity, doubt; leave issues with self-esteem behind. For now you are just wisdom, guidance, magic and knowledge. It is only when you become a sage can you truly understand all the lessons yet to know.

"The cloak I gave each of you is the symbol of you coming of age, of old age, of the path being cleared from the pitfalls that waylay the young. Now your path is absolute truth."

He pointed to two horses. I knew they were for us. As I climbed in the saddle, for the first time in all my visions, I felt like a man. Not a boy. Strange that in the realm of man, at the point of old age you feel useless but in the realm of magic I felt my most powerful. As I spurred on my stead...flash! I was back in the realm of man.

You can make of this vision what you will, but for me it pointed out that it is when you are young, you have to deal with all sorts of different emotions. They can build up so much they just get in the way of everything. Only when you are old are you truly of value as a sage, to give council, to offer advice.

We must recognize this in our world, for a civilization that shuts its old folks away as if they have no purpose is doomed to fail from stupidity. They should be embraced, for they are the lessons and teachings gathered together from the whole of their lives. This is a wasted pool of wisdom, a vast vat of knowledge to be tapped into.

LAGUZ (lah-gooz)

Mystical: Love and emotions

Mythical: Water and dreams/The Leek

Magical: Adapt to your environment

STORY TWENTY-FOUR:

ING

MY ENCOUNTERS WITH THIS RUNE go way, way back. I have always been like the character in the book *Peter Pan* who chased all over the world in search of an easy, carefree life. If you could bottle the power of Ing, you would be a millionaire but too much of it can drive you (and those around you) to insanity.

Before I found this path, I could not stand being bored, so I would seek out adventure and excitement, no matter what chaos it created. Now upon my shamanic way, I am never bored. Today, instead, I go inwards to see what the reason is for Hagal's grip on me, held back by the Gatekeeper until I understand the question posed. There is always something to learn.

With Ing there are a thousand stories I could share, and 90 percent of those would be based around the negative aspects of this rune. Although they are positive, exciting and humorous tales they do not lead to understanding of the rune. It took me 40 years or so to understand its power myself.

I wrote about Gwynn Ap Nudd earlier. He is the Fairy King who lives beneath the Tor. In the histories, St. Collen, one of the first Christian monks to arrive in Avalon, had an encounter with the Lord of the Fae. This monk, who lived as a hermit in a cave at the base of the Tor, was invited to feast with the King of the Fae. The priest smuggled in a bottle of holy water, drove the faeries away and claimed the Tor for the Abbey and Christ. They built a church upon the Tor as a sign of the power of Christianity, but an earthquake knocked most of it down and now only the tower remains. So the Tor sits halfway between the two worlds.

My first encounter with Gwynn was at the Dragon's Egg. I had discovered this place by it being mentioned to me by the strange lady in the first chapter. She did not say where it was, only that it was the high seat of the Fairy King. The crows that I fed at the top of the Tor led me to it when the time was right.

Once again it was early dawn but this was no brilliant sunrise of swirling mists. The sky was pissing it down and the path was slippery as fuck (if you have ever been there, you will know that in the wet weather, it is a steep and treacherous mud bath). I felt blessed to have been shown it by the ravens, although I could have slipped over the side at any moment. I hung tight onto a clump of grass, to help me keep my footing whilst I waited for the permission to enter. Hugwynn, a crow, flew out of the drizzle and landed in the Hawthorne tree that marks the entrance. He cawed and his voice echoed through the damp sky. I knew instinctively that it was the call that heralded my entrance to this holy shrine.

I moved forward with respect. At one point, I slipped and landed flat on my face. Then I gathered my up my offerings that were scattered around and carried on. Finally, my hands reached out and touched the Egg, and a feeling of welcome, of homecoming, washed over me. I placed my muddy offerings on the stone and said prayers, thanking the gods for leading me to this sacred venue. To some, this might just be a rock on the side of a hill, which is like saying Stonehenge is just a few bricks left by some ancient builders. This place is holy. The energy there vibrated through to the core of me.

I sat on the stone, one hand flat on the cold moist surface of the Egg, the other holding my sacred knife, which I had stuck into the sodden earth. My knife would keep me grounded and not allow my soul to travel too far from my body. I stared out across the grey, shadowy horizon and saw a heavy downpour heading my way.

Then his voice came to me, not what I expected at all. It was a sort of Errol Flynn-ish, landed gentry, cross buccaneer accent. "So you found me at last little brother. I have waited a long time for your return. Did you enjoy your travels and pirate adventures?"

I did not reply but sat frozen still, in total awe of this encounter.

The voice continued: "There are many things for you to catch up on, whilst your education has been put aside and you played at life. Never mind, I will soon remedy that. Come inside and let your first lesson begin. A test, so to speak."

The rock beneath my arse became soft and squishy, like a marshmallow. The stone engulfed itself around me and I sunk down deep within the Tor.

I landed on what felt like a cobblestone path. It was dark, very dark. Then he was there once more holding a flaming torch. Due to the buccaneering tone of his voice, I was expecting to see a pirate but to me Gwynn Ap Nudd appeared as I can only say like Laurence Llewelyn Bowen. For those of you who don't recognize that name, Bowen is a flamboyant English interior designer, a dandy of the highest order. That is how Gwynn Ap Nudd always appears to me, but his image will be somewhat different to any who get to have the honour of his presence and the privilege of him enriching their life.

Gwynn Ap Nudd said, "Take this torch and venture down into the darkness. If you turn back with fear, that is OK. If you continue on until the end, that is also OK. Both outcomes will lead to a new future. Nothing is set in stone. The Tor will let you experience that which you need to see or feel. Two words of advice: *be bold.*" Gwynn leapt away into the dark and I was left completely alone in the vaulted bowels of the Tor.

Step-by-step I walked deeper and deeper into the depths of the earth. It was damp and cold up top. This was a different kind of cold, it was bone chilling and dank, and I was glad I had the warmth of the torch for company. No sooner had that thought entered my mind than my only source of heat and light sputtered and went out. I was suffocated by the complete and utter darkness as the last red embers of the torch faded away and a blanket of blackness smothered me.

It always amazes me how quickly the other senses take over in a situation like this. My hearing became acute and the sound of my breath was deafening. My fingers edged their way around every crack and crevice on the tunnel wall and my nose sniffed the chilled, earthy air trying to decipher each and every odour that surrounded me. A strange musky smell—something I have never smelled before—heralded a deep groaning that was resonating ahead of me in the blackness.

I could see a distant faint glimmer of light, which drove back the darkness. A small flicker of hope returned to my heart. The light seemed to waddle and sway from side to side in perfect timing to the sound, a sort of slow, steady *hoom...hoom...hoom.*

The sound brought to mind a noise that might be made by someone or something so heavy that it struggled to move and each step was an effort. The way the light bounced off the walls ahead, I could tell I was approaching a corner and that this thing would come into my space from the other side. We would very soon meet face-to-face.

I stopped dead as the *hoom...hoom...hoom* sound rounded the corner. It was the biggest fucking crocodile I had ever seen—not that I have seen many this close up. The beast was a shining, brilliant, radiant gold. His short, stubby armored legs struggled to drag his humongous belly across the floor. Emerald green eyes peered at me. I was about to high tail it back from whence I had come but within those eyes I saw no malice, no anger, and, no interest in me whatsoever.

I pressed myself flat against the wall and the fat croc just passed me by. As the light that beamed from his scaly skin faded behind me, a pinprick of daylight could be seen as I peered around the corner and I made my way towards it. The dark gave way to the comforting grey tones of my world above. It's not often I can say that I was glad to see a dismal, damp morning, but I was filled with joy as I returned to Midgard.

Outside once more, I took a deep breath of the soggy air.

There was Gwynn reclining on the stone. "Well then little brother, what did you learn from that escapade?"

During my ordeal I hadn't much thought about the lesson I was to learn but as I was asked the question, the answer just flowed out. "Not every creature I meet in the darkness means me harm and to some I am completely irrelevant. Nothing golden will ever harm me, for I am one with the Tor and this is my home but also the home to all sorts of strange and wonderful creatures."

"Excellent, not bad at all, my brother. I can see you are a fast learner. You will need to be, for there is a vast amount of wisdom this land has to offer and not all of it can be absorbed here. Be gone now, but return soon. I have enjoyed your company. Fare thee well, little man."

Gwynn was gone and I was left alone at the Egg. He had called me brother as if I was his kin and that alone gave me a warm sense of belonging.

I had always used my Ing energy in the past to enchant, trick or fool people. Always to get what I wanted. Since my shamanic awakening, I was encountering it in a new way, as a learning aspect, a wise councilor to help me understand more about myself. I still chase pots of gold and seek out rainbows whenever I can but now try to distinguish between self-indulgence and true need.

This force of Ing that dwells within me is what I use to help others get motivated and get things started. It can be harnessed as a positive force to enable the less able to move on, as the perfect catalyst for change, the spark of life that lights the fires of ambition.

INGAZ (in-ga-zu)
Mystical: Action/Inspiration
Mythical: The god Frey/Vitality
Magical: The serpent shedding skin to become bigger

STORY TWENTY-FIVE: OTHEL

I HAVE TO BE VERY SELECTIVE with which adventure I use to illustrate the power of this rune, as some are only meant for my eyes or ears. I have mentioned several stories with Odin already, but the one I will share now is very fresh in my mind and made my path in the United States somewhat clearer.

I had struggled for months to find the right place to connect with spirit at this new location. There were many encounters with land wights and forest beings but nowhere had I felt a place of peace or sanctuary. That was until I got myself a dog. I named her Boudica; Boo for short. She was a Mastiff mix puppy and she gave me the energy and the initiative to go out further in to the wilder areas of my new home.

Each morning I took her on her daily walk, to burn off as much of her puppy power as possible. We ventured further and further afield, until one day we came upon a roaring waterfall. Tall and ancient Douglas firs that reached up for the sky, like long elegant fingers, surrounded the falls. I instantly knew that this was a place I could connect with spirit.

I stood on the rocks that overlooked the falls and chanted my Galdr at the top of my voice. I chanted the chant of Tirwaz, to honour my clan.

Each day, each time, each chant the energy got stronger and more powerful. I felt the spirits of the trees beginning to watch me. The spirits of the long-gone natives listened to me and understood my prayers and the intent of my offerings.

Then for the first time in this new land I felt Odin look upon me and I clearly heard his voice.

I built an altar to honour my gods at this spot but each day when I returned it had been smashed up and cast into the deep pool at the base where the water tumbled over the rocks. I remembered that the same situation arose when I'd built a place of offering on the Tor and asked Odin to show me where I should pray and leave my gifts, a place where others would leave them in peace.

A redheaded woodpecker flew out of the trees, landed on a nearby stone and marked what I thought was the chosen spot. The woodpecker, as a symbol, indicates a place of protection from a coming storm, a place to wait it out until the sun returns.

As I laid out the nine sticks on the ground to make my helruna (a geometric shape that represents the nine worlds which, when combined, make the 24 runes of the Elder Futhark), Boo barged past me and scattered the wooden staves all over the fucking place. The last one had fallen into a deep crevice between two of the huge river rocks. I scrambled on my belly, stretching every sinew of my muscles to retrieve it. As I did, a ray of sun broke through the clouds and lit up a huge boulder on the path above, which stood between two majestic redwoods. Sitting in the branches of one and cawing loudly were a pair of jet-black ravens.

All these events had combined to show me my place of connection and I made my way back up from the falls. This time Boo sat still as I completed my symbol beneath the rock. As I intoned the final rune and the sound faded into the forest, Odin spoke to me. "Be proud, be loud and be clear. Show them that their ancestors are watching and are happy with this work. I will be with you and we shall wake up their hearts."

I knew what he meant and what he wanted me to do.

Tara and I were to attend the Junction City Scandinavian Festival that weekend. On three of the four days of the event, I was to give a talk on the runes.

The first talk was to six people when I first started and grew to ten by the time I finished. One of them visited our booth later and was in dire need of some runic help.

At the second talk I gave, there were a dozen people at the start and maybe thirty by the end. Each of the talks was to show the relevance of the runes in our modern language and explain the phonetic meaning of each rune and to unravel the names carved on Viking swords, so that the layman could understand the reason behind the name. Near the end of the talk I was asking people to give their names so I could reveal the hidden runic meaning within.

From the attending crowd, just by shouting out randomly, I could see what they did for a living and talk about their personalities. This I had never done before and it was eerie, but accurate. On the final few names just as I finished the talk, I felt my voice change. It dropped a couple of octaves and it was Odin who thanked the folks for listening to his wisdom.

Back at my booth one member of the audience came up to me and thanked me for the lesson. He told me that he was a member of a local kindred, that it was so good to hear about the runes spoken in a way that the general populace could connect with them. I explained that for me, the runes belonged to everyone not just a select few, they dwell within us, in our daily lives and in our language.

At the third and final talk, a gathering of sixty or more people awaited my wisdom. This time my words flowed with ease. Each rune's energy hovered above the audience as I explained how it resonated within in our modern world and gave a short version of the legends behind each symbol. By the time I had got to Tyr I was in full bardic flow and the story of the losing of his hand to the wolf Fenris enchanted my audience. I don't really remember the rest of the runes that I talked about, all I know is that it was Odin who spoke the sacred prayer—not myself— and tears were streaming down my face by the end of his recital.

The words of the Tyrwaz chant were used, but not the chants. It went as follows:

> I call to my ancestors back to the beginning of time,
> my Father's Father's Father,
> those who came before me.
> Know that I honour you in my life,
> I sing your songs and tell your stories.
> Your blood flows in my veins and I will not forget.
> Hail the sacred ancestors.
> I call to my Brother and Sisters of this time,
> the keepers of the beacon fire.
> We are the link in the chain from the past to the future.
> We must be strong, we will be strong, we are strong.
> Hail my Brothers and Sisters of this time.

I call to my descendants until the end of time,
my children's children's children,
those who come after us.
Remember us who came before,
Sing our songs, tell our stories.
For you are the realization of all our hopes
and all our dreams.
Hail the sacred descendants.

I stood at the centre of the stage, more tears welling in my eyes and spoke now in my own words. "Hail Lord Odin, the All Father, the giver of knowledge, the seeker of wisdom."

I was expecting those gathered to be freaked out, but instead they gave me a standing ovation, not for me but Odin himself, for it was he who they listened to that day.

You can make of this tale what you want, but it is a thin line made of humanity's generations that links us all, which is my key to the Odinic rune. It is not the things that make us different, but the things that make us the same. We are one tribe, one people, one species, living in this one very special world, in Midgard, the realm of man. Odin is the thread that holds us together and links us through time and space to the past and the future.

"Hail Odin!"

OTHEL (oth-el-oh)

Mystical: Family/Authority

Mythical: Odin, Father of All

Magical: The sleeping Dragon/
Our life's treasures

STORY TWENTY-SIX:

DAEGAZ

THIS IS THE ADVENTURE THAT came to pass on the summer solstice in 2011. From early June onwards, strange characters were turning up in the town. Keep in mind, Glastonbury is a town of a bloody lot of strange characters and I suppose, to an outsider, I would be classed as one of them. Tim and I were very aware of an uncomfortable presence building, engulfing the town in its energy as the month progressed on.

One early morning, I was making my way to my place of vision, amongst the bramble bushes of the Faerie wood which nestled in the valley at the bottom of the Tor. It was no later than six o'clock and I had just started my vision chants, when I heard a rustle in the bushes, maybe 10 yards away. The ravens cawed in my head, they warned me of strangers. I turned in the direction of the disturbance.

Between the branches of a lush green beech tree in its full summer foliage, I could see on the steep bank above me an elderly man, maybe late 70s, standing stark, bollock naked and staring in my direction. An equally naked elderly woman then joined him. She pulled a jumper over her head and passed a piece of clothing to her partner.

Together they quickly dressed and scampered away followed by a yellow dog (a pale beige Labrador). I think that I had scared the fuck out of them and rudely interrupted whatever they were up to.

Something was definitely not right about this pair and I proceeded to focus the attention of my vision work on their antics and the local energetic unrest. Strange things were definitely afoot.

I shook my bells, called in the handmaidens, summoned the ravens, the wolves and the badgers to watch over me and slipped into the world of trance.

Goll came quickly, jingling along on his caribou and joined me at the council fire. Most of my other guides were already there and all gathered round the shaman as he emptied the contents of his medicine bag on the dusty floor.

"White bear rattle!" he said as he picked up his medicine tool and shook it at me. "Quickly boy, shift your shape and follow those demons. Use the energy of bear but shape of raven and stalk them from above."

The other guides chanted or banged sticks together as I took on the form of a white crow, left my body and flew up higher and higher into the sky. This was another of those visions-within-a-vision, and things were happening really fast. From my high vantage point above the Tor, I caught sight of the elderly couple and the dog as they headed across the field and back to town.

Both must have felt my energy and turned towards me. Their eyes were completely dark, black as coal. Goll was right; these were demons. The shadow of something dark and menacing blocked out the sun above and behind me. I crooked my neck back as I hovered in the swirling winds that swept off the sides of the Tor.

Whoosh! Swoop!

A huge black griffin mobbed me and sent me tumbling down towards the grassy bank below.

As soon as my wings made contact with the ground, I shifted instantly into white bear and smashed the griffin hard across his beak. I'd sent him fleeing for safety with one swipe of my paw. I glanced over to the couple once more, who themselves had shifted into black wolves or werewolves as they made their escape they ran on their hind legs as if still human. I turned and cantered back down the Tor and returned to my waiting body at the council fire.

"They are demons Goll! Werewolf demons! What the hell do I do?" I sat and waited for my teacher's guidance. There was a long pause where not a sound was spoken.

Goll's mind was somewhere else.

Then he returned to us and spoke. "A portal has been opened here which allows these dark entities to enter. That is the energy you have felt rising in the town. It must be closed as the sun rises on Solstice. You will use the power of that moment, the chanting of Daegaz, the sanctuary of the Egg, to focus the Sun's rays as it is born anew on the brightest day. Your chant will help to drive them from this place and back into the dark from whence they came. Now away with you; there is much to do."

I left my vision spot and headed back to town. I kept my eyes open for the spooky couple but they were nowhere to be seen. As I opened the final cattle gate on the way down, a pale coloured Lab barged past me and charged like a bat out of hell down the road. Just for one second it gazed at me with its jet-black eyes.

I texted Tim: "Tea, bro. Need to talk. Shit's happening!"

Tim's reply was: "Bang fucking on, bro!"

We met at the Coffee Bean, which no longer exists, in the Gauntlet alleyway. I explained my experiences in the Faerie wood. Things had not been happening only to me. Tim also had received instructions from spirit; our friend Gary had as well. As the sun rose on the Solstice, I would be on the Tor, Gary at Brent Knoll (an ancient Iron Age hill fort) about twenty miles away and Tim would be at an undisclosed location that only he and spirit knew.

As Solstice approached, the energy in the town went haywire. There were mad punch-ups in the streets after the pubs turned out. Some loony person was beating people up and threatening tourists at the White Spring. An abundance of crazies and vampire Goths migrated from the cities to our sleepy Somerset market town, all being fuelled by the high point of midsummer.

It was about three a.m. on the Solstice morning as I left the comfort of my bed and made my way up the back way to the Tor. I walked the path of my sacred walk and connected with all the spiritual places that I passed by. As I ambled along beneath the archway of Hazel trees that make the roof of the Faerie lane, the distant drumming from the revellers atop the Tor could be heard. Every now and then the orange glow from the flickering of open fires caught my eye. The speckled light dotted the morning twilight.

When I am doing medicine, I avoid crowds as much as possible. At the major festivals of the year, it is impossible to have complete solitude, especially at the sacred energy spots and I was heading for the Egg stone.

Even before I rounded the corner and the Egg came into sight, I could hear rave music, laughter and shouting. I was not surprised to find half a dozen partygoers doing their thing at the Dragon's Egg. I had a massive urge to turn back and find a more solitary venue, but this is where I was supposed to be and nowhere else would do. I took a deep breath, called to Gwynn, the Faerie King, as I asked permission to enter.

An owl's hoot echoed through in the woods below. That was my cue. I was being heralded and welcomed to the festivities. I was really close before the mob of pissheads heard the jingling of my bells. As I ducked under the branches of the Hawthorn to enter, the drunken barrage began.

"Whayhay! It's a fucking wizard! Join us, Harry Potter."

"That's not Harry, that's Dumbledor."

"You're both fucking wrong! It's Gandalph you knob-jockies!"

"Leave him be, let him do his stuff. I think it's sweet."

I honestly prefer having the piss taken out of me by the lads, than being patronized by some soppy, half-cut teenage girl.

Nevertheless I entered their fray and claimed my space. I sat at the edge of the group with my back against a rock, faced the east to welcome the new dawn. Then I lit some mugwort.

"Is that ganja, grandad? Can we have some?" said the oldest boy who had the faint hint of a scouse (from Liverpool) accent.

I ignored the remarks of my youthful company, gave offerings, took out my drum, cleansed it with the swirling smoke and began to drum.

At first I played slowly and softly, then faster and faster and much louder. Totally losing myself in the rhythm and blocking out the din from their iPod speaker. My chanting became automatic, a variation on the Galdr of Daegaz, to heal the land and purge the darkness with the rising of the dawn. A deep resonate intoning that vibrated through my chest and amplified out of the chamber of the drum as I held it sideways against my chest.

"DAEGAZ-OO-NAAAH."

Over and over and again I roard until the chant and the drum became one.

I could feel the power rising, evoking the light. It emanated all around me. I was totally encompassed in a ball of pure brilliance. As the sun finally sneaked a peek over the horizon, I released the energy and let it rush out over the land like a wave, a tsunami of cleansing light.

I shouted out and called to the gods. "All Father see my prayer, know my will and aid my task. Hail Lord Odin!"

I snapped out of my trance almost immediately to be faced by a group of gobsmacked kids, of which one lad bravely spoke up. "Heavy fucking shit man. Are you like the real deal or what?"

There was no real answer to that question.

I gathered up my things, spat on the ground, wished then a happy Solstice and left to go to a different place to watch the sun come up.

It was truly a glorious sunrise, with beams of red gold and yellow forking across the sky. As I made my way up to the top to say hello to some of my friends from the town, the haunting face of a beast appeared in the morning clouds, a werewolf. The image stared down, giving me one last glance before it was washed away by the approaching day. I knew that what others and I had done that morning had worked. The air felt fresh, clean and the town could breathe again.

Once again, I am not really bothered about whether you believe me or not. As you have gotten this far in the book, I expect you are open minded enough to find the wisdom within each tale.

This was the awakening of Daegaz within me, showing me my own power, to have faith in my own abilities. I was able to overcome distractions, ridicule and focus on the work at hand, to see it through to completion. I was able to bring about the dramatic change Daegaz can generate, that transition from caterpillar to butterfly, from night to day.

DAEGAZ (day-garz)
Mystical: Transition/Change
Mystical: Dawning of a new time
Magical: To seek knowledge in the extremes, but to not be an extremist

CONCLUSION

T HIS BOOK WAS TO BE a how-to-read-the-runes manual, but after consulting with Odin, that intention changed. My mission now is to let the reader know how the runes changed my life and maybe get you excited enough to take up the challenge yourself. Before you do, I just want to leave you with some thoughts and a simple example of a vision.

"Only ever say, do, or go where or what the runes show you."

WARNING: YOU CANNOT READ RUNES FOR EVERYONE. TO THINK YOU CAN IS EGO, AND EGO HAS NOTHING TO DO WITH READING THE RUNES. ALSO YOU HAVE NO RIGHT TO READ THE RUNES FOR OTHERS UNTIL YOU YOURSELF LIVE LIFE BY THEIR GUIDANCE.

I will now grab three runes at random from my pouch and vision on them, so the gods can show you how this works.

Three chosen runes are:

JARA   SOWELO   HAGEL

These are three runes I just picked at random from my pouch. Strangely enough, it appears to indicate a delay in the work I love, but the meaning should be irrelevant to you at the moment.

So first I call in my spirit guides. I chant my chants of protection and open the veil between the realms. This vision journey takes me to a land of plenty. I walk through a lush wheat field that has just started to be harvested. I watch as the farmers gather the crop under the golden shining sun.

Just as all seems well, a storm moves in. A crazy hailstorm. I stand and shiver under an oak tree with the sodden farm workers. They wonder if there will be enough of the crop left, after the violent downpour, to last through winter. Then, in the distance, I hear the blast of Heimdal's horn, calling me for council.

At the place of the gatekeeper, at the entrance onto Bifrost, the rainbow bridge that leads to Asgard, I wait for his guidance.

Wait is the appropriate word. I wait and I wait for what seems like an age, then he emerges out of the dark fog that hangs swirling over the bridge.

"Prepare for hard times, nothing you have not been through before. Think of how much stronger you became after your last ordeal, how much greater your connection to spirit has become." His booming voice echoes in my head then fades away.

Back at the oak tree I talk of Heimdal's words and say that the farm workers must make do this winter. They must find warmth in each other's company; although their bellies will grumble and be empty, their hearts will stay full of love. It is the bad times that make people appreciate the good times even more.

In this vision, I gained wisdom for myself and also passed on the guidance of the gods to others. Were the farmers just part of the vision or were they in another realm and called on the answers to their plight from a shaman spirit?

From just taking three runes, not knowing what they would show me, these are two bits of wisdom I gained:

- *Allow your mind to be free, just let the source of the runes flow through you.*
- *Let Odin take you by the hand and help you write your own holy book, showing you a better way.*

As I have mentioned several times before, each man or woman's runic journey is completely their own. What joy and coming together of minds when two of us meet up and discuss our own experiences with each individual rune.

There are at least two runes with which I often use somebody else's experience as an example during a reading. This is more important when you are reading for the opposite sex. Even though people must embrace both male and female energy on our quests, it is good for me to get a female perspective of runic energy. Some people's stories you will resonate with some will have no relevance to you at all. This all good and exactly how it should be.

Our quest is a road of wisdom and the more we talk and share, the greater the well of knowledge we can draw from. Tim and I discuss for hours our vision meanings and lessons of each rune. We listen with respect to each other's tales, and take from it that which we can use to increase the wealth of our own medicine bag. So by sharing, we have both become wiser. Odin yearned for wisdom so much he was willing to give his eye for it.

It is not the way of a rune walker to accept the words in another's book but to seek a greater understanding than those who came before. We can follow in their footsteps but each generation must take a few more steps of their own.

Our runic path as a people has been blocked by dogma for centuries, it is only now at the beginning of the twenty first century that the road ahead is clear.

As I finished this book, I asked Odin to let me see a vision, with which to share with the readers of this tale. This is the message he wants you to understand, to help you connect with his energy. I closed my eyes and called on Odin.

> "All Father, one eyed wise one. Odin of the Aesir.
> Come thought, come memory, come Odin."

I dipped my hand deep in my rune pouch and pulled out three runes. I called out loud.

"My Lord what is it you need to say?"

These were the runes I was given:

WYNN   ANSUZ   SOWELO

Now I allowed the energy to work though me and show me the message for the readers. I allowed myself to be taken over, to let the All Father write the final words of this book, for he had shown me Ansuz and that is the voice of the All Father. So, I will let him speak.
"Blessings, to all who find new life in the old ways."

Jeremy R J White

The words below are the words of Odin that came to me though his channeled energy. At no point should they be edited in any way.

See my runes, feel my message. All you have to do is call, to speak up and I will answer. Advance from beyond the mists so that I may recognize you, that I may see your battle flag and remember when it hung in my hall. My words are simple, as the truth should be. It is an easy path to follow, the one that leads to truth, truth in your words, truth in your actions, truth in your heart. Ignore my wisdom if you wish, but my knowledge has been hard fought. The blood of your ancestors back to the beginning has flowed down the rivers of time, so that you may stand in this moment. Do not waste their sacrifice, stand in the sun, the golden light of my son Baldr and be truly happy.

ABOUT THE AUTHOR

Jeremy R J White was born in 1963 just outside of London, England to Barry and Rona White, scrap metal dealers and horse traders. He had a glorious childhood, living in both the home counties and Wales. Magic was all around him but never spoken of in public.

At the age of 19, he got a job in a shady West End casino and from there his life took on a gypsy existence. He traveled the world, setting up and working in gaming establishments for a variety of rather dubious characters.

In 1996, he became seriously ill and gave up the casino work. Upon recovery, he managed his father's pub, then left to start his own business running corporate events such as paintballing, Four-by-Four days out, casino- and James Bond-themed weekends. The deals got dodgier and dodgier until 2006, when this 'house of cards' collapsed.

He divorced, lost his home and the ability to live with his three beautiful children. Thoughts of suicide entered his mind; love for his family prevented the act. It was then and only then did he clearly hear the voice of spirit. He heard Odin. It was he who came to White in a vision, grabbed him by the scruff of the neck and told him he had work to do. White had been interested in psychic phenomena since childhood but kept it secret and hidden. It was only when he had lost everything that could be what he always had known he was: A SHAMAN.

Jeremy White and Tim Raven in the Abbey.

Jeremy R J White

Spiritual Guide ~ Psychic ~ Healer ~ Teacher

Offering:
Walking with Wizards – Guided Walks of Avalon

Online:
Walking the Nine Worlds Journey Class • Awakening with the
Runes Classes • Northern Shamanic Studies Classes • Rune
Readings • Shamanic Healings • Spiritual Counsel • Blessings •
Ceramic Art • Custom Made Rune Sets • Talismans

www.JeremyRJWhite.com

CPSIA information can be obtained
at www.ICGtesting.com
Printed in the USA
LVHW050138060819
626568LV00021B/1922/P